Travel Guide for Kids

Mystery Adventure Tour of London

Elizabeth Anne

© **Copyright 2024 - All rights reserved.**

The content contained within this book may not be reproduced, duplicated or transmitted without direct written permission from the author or the publisher.

Under no circumstances will any blame or legal responsibility be held against the publisher, or author, for any damages, reparation, or monetary loss due to the information contained within this book, either directly or indirectly.

Legal Notice:

This book is copyright protected. It is only for personal use. You cannot amend, distribute, sell, use, quote or paraphrase any part, or the content within this book, without the consent of the author or publisher.

Disclaimer Notice:

Please note the information contained within this document is for educational and entertainment purposes only. All effort has been executed to present accurate, up to date, reliable, complete information. No warranties of any kind are declared or implied. Readers acknowledge that the author is not engaged in the rendering of legal, financial, medical or professional advice. The content within this book has been derived from various sources. Please consult a licensed professional before attempting any techniques outlined in this book.

By reading this document, the reader agrees that under no circumstances is the author responsible for any losses, direct or indirect, that are incurred as a result of the use of the information contained within this document, including, but not limited to, errors, omissions, or inaccuracies.

TABLE OF CONTENTS

INTRODUCTION 1
    WHAT YOU NEED TO DO 2

CHAPTER 1: THE INTRUDER AT THE CABINET OFFICE 5
    INTRODUCTION 5
        The UK: Lay of the Land 5
        London: A Mosaic of Places and People 6
        The Letter 7
        The Game Is On! 8
    THE MINISTERIAL OFFICES 8
        The Cabinet Office 8
        The Prime Minister's Home and Office 10
        Fun and Trivia Questions 11
        Riddles 12
    THE LONDON EYE 13
        Fun and Trivia Questions 15
        Riddles 15
    BIG BEN AND THE HOUSES OF PARLIAMENT 16
        Big Ben 16
        The Houses of Parliament: Palace of Westminster 17
        Fun and Trivia Questions 18
        Riddles 19
    THE BIG REVEAL 19
    SUMMARY 20

CHAPTER 2: WHY IS THE FUTURE OF LONDON CITY IN JEOPARDY? 21
    INTRODUCTION 21
        The City: Days of Yore 21
        The Threat 22
        The Game is Afoot 22
    THE SQUARE MILE 23
        Fun and Trivia Questions 25
        Riddles 26
    THE STUDIO OF MAGIC 28
        Fun and Trivia Questions 29
        Riddles 29
    THE STONE OF BRUTUS: THE HEART OF LONDON 30
        Fun and Trivia Questions 31
        Riddle 32
    THE BIG REVEAL 32
    SUMMARY 32

CHAPTER 3: THE MYSTERY OF THE TRAPPED TOURISTS 33
    INTRODUCTION 33
        The City: Greenery and Nature 33
        The Problem 34
        Buckle Up! 35

Scotland Yard	35
Fun and Trivia Questions	*36*
Riddles	*36*
Britain's Valhalla	37
Fun and Trivia Questions	*38*
Riddles	*39*
The Garden of the Abbey and Convent	39
Fun and Trivia Questions	*40*
Riddles	*41*
The Big Reveal	41
Summary	41

CHAPTER 4: THE MYSTERY OF SAVING THE BRITISH MONARCHY 43

Introduction	43
The City: Coins and Cash	*43*
The Case	*44*
Let It Roll!	*44*
The East End and Whitechapel	45
Fun and Trivia Questions	*47*
Riddles	*47*
The Wall and Tower Hill	48
Fun and Trivia Questions	*49*
Riddles	*49*
The Bridge and the Royal Fortress	50
Fun and Trivia Questions	*51*
Riddles	*52*
The Big Reveal	53
Summary	53

CHAPTER 5: UNCOVERING THE SECRET UNDERGROUND DRUG TRANSPORT IN LONDON 55

Introduction	55
The City: Gallivanting About	*55*
The Mystery	*57*
Chin Up!	*57*
The Royal London Residence	58
Fun and Trivia Questions	*60*
Riddles	*60*
The First Public National Museum	61
Fun and Trivia Questions	*63*
Riddles	*63*
The Two Museums	63
London Transport Museum	*63*
The Postal Museum	*64*
Fun and Trivia Questions	*65*
Riddles	*66*
The Big Reveal	66
Summary	66

CONCLUSION 67

TRIVIA AND FUN ANSWERS 69

CHAPTER 1: TRIVIA AND FUN ANSWERS 71

The Ministerial Offices	71
The London Eye	72
Big Ben and the Houses of Parliament	72

CHAPTER 2: TRIVIA AND FUN ANSWERS 74
THE SQUARE MILE 74
THE STUDIO OF MAGIC 74
THE STONE OF BRUTUS: THE HEART OF LONDON 75

CHAPTER 3: TRIVIA AND FUN ANSWERS 77
SCOTLAND YARD 77
BRITAIN'S VALHALLA 78
THE GARDEN OF THE ABBEY AND CONVENT 78

CHAPTER 4: TRIVIA AND FUN ANSWERS 80
EAST END AND WHITE CHAPEL 80
THE WALL AND TOWER HILL 81
THE BRIDGE AND THE ROYAL FORTRESS 81

CHAPTER 5: TRIVIA AND FUN ANSWERS 83
THE ROYAL LONDON RESIDENCE 83
THE FIRST PUBLIC NATIONAL MUSEUM 83
THE MUSEUMS 84

ANSWERS TO THE MYSTERY 86
CHAPTER 1 86
CHAPTER 2 86
CHAPTER 3 87
CHAPTER 4 87
CHAPTER 5 88

ABOUT THE AUTHOR 89

REFERENCES 91

ANNEXURE: MORE FUN PLACES TO HANG OUT 97
CHAPTER 1: THE INTRUDER AT THE CABINET OFFICE 98
Eateries *98*
Parks and Green Spots *99*
Fun, Entertainment, and Education *99*
CHAPTER 2: WHY IS THE FUTURE OF LONDON CITY IN JEOPARDY? 100
Eateries *100*
Parks and Green Spots *100*
Fun, Entertainment, and Education *100*
CHAPTER 3: THE MYSTERY OF THE TRAPPED TOURISTS 101
Eateries *101*
Parks and Green Spots *102*
Fun, Entertainment, and Education *102*
CHAPTER 4: THE MYSTERY OF SAVING THE BRITISH MONARCHY 102
Eateries *102*
Parks and Green Spots *103*
Fun, Entertainment, and Education *104*
CHAPTER 5: UNCOVERING THE SECRET UNDERGROUND DRUG TRANSPORT IN LONDON 105
Eateries *105*
Parks and Green Spots *105*
Fun, Entertainment, and Education *105*

INTRODUCTION

Have you always wanted to travel and visit continents, countries, and cities far from home? Do you dream of meeting new people, tasting different foods, and taking part in cultures not your own? Have you also wanted to be a detective like Sherlock Holmes, sleuthing your way into finding clues, unmasking villains, preventing murders, and solving problems? Then you have picked up the right book.

Travel Guide for Kids: Mystery Adventure Tour of London is part of a series of books, called *The Globe Trotter Detectives*, for travel detectives like you. This book is a traveler's guide to London, but not for the faint-hearted. You will explore the wonders of big and historic London while unraveling clues about mysteries and crimes happening in the city! These are not your everyday mysteries but those based on myths about London. Not only will you be a regular tourist but also a mystery solver of the highest degree! Now, who can beat that offer?

What You Need to Do

In each chapter, you will find plenty of trivia questions about parts of the city. Whenever you feel the urge to check, the answers are provided on the last page of this book. When you are done trying to crack them, you can just flip over and locate the answers.

Are you thinking this may turn out to be a textbook (oh, so boring!) in disguise? Fear not! Every chapter has a hidden surprise for you—a whole juicy mystery to sink your teeth into. These mysteries will be found in one or the other myths surrounding the places you visit. You will be the ultimate globe-trotting detective!

As you move from one place to the next in London, put on your thinking caps and:

- watch out for clues leading to the heart of the mystery buried in the chapter.

- differentiate between the red herrings and the real clues. While the first will have you barking up the wrong tree (following the wrong lead), the second will take you one step closer to the solution.

- lastly, though these may not help you solve the mystery, watch out for those fascinating and strange English expressions, terms, and words (with their meanings in brackets) scattered all over this book that will help you understand British English better.

Don't forget to refer to the Annexure at the end of the book where you will find more fun places, eateries, shopping centers, and much more in and around the main places you visit.

As a detective, you will have to be quick in your reasoning and nimble of imagination to move from one place to the next. Well, you can't fly, but you can certainly close your eyes, think, and dream. You can travel the length and breadth of the city mentally to find answers to your burning questions. I encourage you to visit the places of each chapter in any order you like but to follow the riddle questions in order of their numbers.

Ensure you take plenty of photos of the places you visit. At times, you may be able to answer the trivia questions on your own by simply observing the place or the building. If you feel there are questions you need help with, reach out to family members or others traveling with you because even the best detectives always had their aides close at hand—Holmes had Watson; Poirot, his faithful Hastings; and even Nancy Drew, her Bess and George!

After the trivia questions related to each location, the riddles will lead you to still more clues, until you ferret out the logical answer. The final answers to the mysteries will only be revealed at the end of the book. Don't be in haste to check out the answers on the last page! After all, what is the life of a detective without some challenge, eh?

So, what are you waiting for, dear travel detective? Let's take this adventure to the next level!

CHAPTER 1:

The Intruder at the Cabinet Office

Introduction

Hello, dear travel detective! Are you ready for our very first mystery in London?

But wait, before we dive in, what do you know about London and where it is? After all, as a globetrotting detective, you need some context about the place before stepping into it.

The UK: Lay of the Land

London is the capital of the United Kingdom (UK). The UK is made up of Northern Ireland and Great Britain, which includes England, Wales, and Scotland. The UK also includes small islands collectively called the British Isles. Except for Northern Ireland, which shares a land border with the Republic of Ireland, the UK is surrounded by water on all sides—the Atlantic Ocean, North Sea, Irish Sea, Celtic Sea, and the English Channel. This is also why Britain is called an "island country". Did you know that England, or Britain, is called "Blighty" just for fun? It was a nickname the soldiers of the world wars popularized.

London: A Mosaic of Places and People

Located in southeastern England, and lying across the River Thames, London is the largest city in the UK. It is also one of the oldest. It was established nearly 2,000 years ago by the Romans, who called it Londinium! You can imagine the number and types of people, cultures, and languages that must have shaped a city so old and vast.

Did you know that over 300 languages, including English, Polish, Bengali, Turkish, French, and plenty more are spoken in London? It has almost 9 million people, while the whole of the UK has a population of 67.6 million. This means that a little more than one in every ten people in the UK are Londoners!

Why is London so important to the UK? It is the main cultural center of the country, one of the most famous tourist destinations in the world, and home to one of the best transportation systems in the world.

Modern London includes the city of London, which is the economic hub of the country with its banks and trading centers, as well as Westminster, the political seat of the country.

But did you know that not everyone was always so enthusiastic about the city? William Cobbett, an 18th-century writer and great nature lover, did not find the industrial town of London poetic or beautiful. He, therefore, nicknamed it the "Great Wen." "Wen" meant a cyst or wart! Thankfully, today London is called the "Foodie Capital" of the world or "Where Royalty Lives."

Enough about London now.

What's this? Is there a letter for you? Oh yes, and an important one it looks like. It has come all the way from the Prime Minister's Office!

Looks like the mystery has found you good and proper (completely or thoroughly)!

The Letter

TOP SECRET

70, Whitehall

Dear _____ *(Feel free to fill your name here)*

Hope this letter finds you in the pink of health (in good health). This is an official invite for you to join us at the Cabinet Office on a secret mission of the utmost importance.

We urgently need your assistance. An unknown intruder has been wandering around our offices, leaving mud and filth everywhere. Though nothing has been stolen yet, we fear for the safety of our country and its precious government documents.

We invite you to use your first-class brain cells to crack the identity of this intruder and bring them to justice!

N.B: This letter is for your eyes only. Burn it after you read it.

The Game Is On!

Well, since you know now what is at stake, let's get going. But before you begin, a quick reminder about the rules:

1. Each location's nearest Tube Station is represented by emoticons you have to work out on your own. The answers to these are provided at the end of the book just before the answers to the trivia questions.

2. Each location you proceed to will have a riddle or two.

3. Some of these riddles will reveal more clues leading to the final mystery. Others will only be red herrings or false clues to confuse you.

4. Gather the riddles and answer them to arrive at the answer.

5. To check the final answer, check out the answers at the end of the book.

6. Apart from the riddles, every location has a few fun questions, giving you more trivia and details about these places. The answers to these are at the end of the book. Don't ignore the trivia questions, as they will strengthen your investigative skills and sharpen your brain so you shine as a fine detective.

So, are you all set? Ready, steady, go!

The Ministerial Offices

Nearest Tube Station: ⬅️ 💂

The Cabinet Office

Location: 70 Whitehall

No need to get your knickers in a twist (get worried or confused) over this one. The "Cabinet Office" of the UK is the name of a department in the UK ministry as well as the name of the building where the department meets most often.

The UK is a monarchy. You may have heard that King Charles III has been newly crowned. However, the UK also has a democratically elected government.

The Cabinet Office includes ministers such as the Prime Minister and other cabinet ministers such as the Deputy Prime Minister, Ministers of State, Secretaries of State, and the Leaders of the two houses of the parliament—the House of Lords and House of Commons.

Look closer at your letter. You will find it has been sent from 70 Whitehall. This building is where many, but not all, of the cabinet meetings take place. It is located right next to the Prime Minister's office and residence.

The Cabinet Hall has not one but several meeting rooms called Cabinet Office Briefing Rooms (COBR), often nicknamed COBRA. To remember the name better, you can think of the hooded, venomous, and deadly snake, the cobra. To date, only a single photo of the COBRA has been released and available, and this was in response to the Freedom of Information Act, 2000.

70 Whitehall, where the Cabinet Office buildings stand today, goes a long way back in history. Once upon a time, these buildings were part of the Palace of Whitehall, which was called the York Palace even before that! In the 16th century, King Henry VIII got the York Palace redesigned and renamed it the Palace of Whitehall. He even used it as one of his main residences in London. Many of William Shakespeare's plays were first performed in the Palace of Whitehall.

In 1698, thankfully when the palace was no longer being used as a royal residence, a careless maidservant accidentally started a fire when she tried to dry linen sheets on a charcoal brazier. It caused almost the entire palace to burn down. Today, within the Cabinet Office, one can still see parts of the old palace intact! If you get the chance to be inside, ensure you try to watch out for this old palace. The only fully surviving section of the Palace of Whitehall is the Banqueting Hall, built in 1622 by one of the first famous English architects, Inigo Jones.

Over the years, the place where the Palace of Whitehall stood was built over with many buildings used for government purposes. "Whitehall" now refers to all these buildings related to the UK Government including the Cabinet Office, Ministry of Defence, and several other important government departments.

Since 70 Whitehall and the adjacent Downing Street are perhaps the most politically important locations of the country, both are heavily guarded. Nobody is allowed inside without a security clearance. In fact, when the gates to Downing Street are closed, the public can't even see House Number 10 on it. However, in 2007, a man named Obadiah Marius and his girlfriend Ms. Smith were able to walk into 70 Whitehall and out of a security door that led to the back entrance of 10 Downing Street. It was only here that they were stopped and questioned by the guards.

The Prime Minister's Home and Office

Location: 10 Downing Street

Close to Whitehall is a small lane, called Downing Street, which is gated and heavily guarded. You must be wondering what all the fuss is about.

Well, in house number 10 on Downing Street lives the Prime Minister. There are as many as 100 rooms in the Prime Minister's house, and it is at least 300 years old. The house has office rooms, too, for all his important work. Do you know there is also a hall in the Prime Minister's house for cabinet meetings? It is called the Cabinet Room of 10 Downing Street.

Though it is one of the most photographed and filmed doors worldwide, normally, nonofficial visitors are not even allowed into Downing Street. It has a gate and guards restricting the entry of the general public.

If you have seen pictures, you will know that 10 Downing Street is known for its signature black walls. Once upon a time, they were ordinary yellow brick walls that became so dirtied by the pollution of smoggy London city that they turned black. It was only in the 1960s, during big renovations, when they discovered the real color of the wall. However, city planners decided to paint the cleaned walls black to maintain the familiar appearance of the house.

Together, the Cabinet Office and the Prime Minister's Office make all the important decisions for the country related to national security, education, health, finance, and more.

Remember the following things before you plan your trip:

- During certain times of the year, with special permission, the Cabinet Office organizes guided tours including a visit to Downing Street.

- Take pictures and videos of yourself outside and as close as possible to these historic buildings.

- If you get close enough, notice the wonky "0" of the number plate of 10 Downing Street. Rumor has it that city officials have always tried to keep up with the original "10" on the door from the olden days, when the "0" was poorly fixed and slightly crooked!

- Just in case you don't get an entry into Downing Street, you have an almost exact replica of the Prime Minister's House ten minutes away at 10 Adam Street, off the Strand. You can get your selfie in front of the famous door after all!

Well, detective, time to sharpen your skills. How many of the following questions do you know the answer to?

Fun and Trivia Questions

1. Do you know for how long British Prime Ministers have stayed at 10 Downing Street? Is it closer to 100 or 300 years?

2. Apart from black, what was the only other color the door of 10 Downing Street was painted? When was this?

3. Who was the British Prime Minister when World War II broke out? Was it Neville Chamberlain or Winston Churchill?

4. Who was the last private or nonpolitical resident of 10 Downing Street? What happened to him? (Hint: His name is shared by a farm bird.)

5. Generally, how many members are there in the UK Cabinet? Is it 5–10 members or 15–25 members?

6. Which of the following countries uses the same or a similar structure of cabinet as the UK—India, Mexico, or Guadalupe?

7. What nickname is often associated with a cabinet—"kitchen cabinet," "pantry cabinet", or "scullery cabinet"? Why do we use this particular term?

8. Apart from the Tube Station you already named, which other Tube Station is near the Cabinet Office? Here's a clue: Cha 💍 ✖

9. What is the UK flag called? Why is it called this?

My dear detective, it is now time for the riddles that hold a clue to the identity of the mystery intruder!

Riddles

Answer the riddles below to name two animals, one of which is related to the intruder.

- **Clue 1:** I'm a magical creature with a horn. I'm not real, but in stories, I'm seen. I'm also found on the UK coat of arms. Who am I?

- **Clue 2:** I played a big role in carrying the Black Death, killing thousands of people in England long ago. Who am I, and what did I carry?

Are you ready for our next location? Let's get going!

The London Eye

Location: Riverside Building, County Hall

Nearest Tube Station: 💧 🚽

The London Eye is a huge observation wheel that gives people a bird's eye view of the city. To give you an idea of its height, it stands 443 ft tall, while the average height of a man is 5 ft and 7–9 inches. It is located on the South Bank of Thames in the Borough of Lambeth.

When it was built in 1999, it was the tallest Ferris wheel in the world. Now it is the fourth largest in the world; there are taller ones in the United States, Singapore, and China. It still holds the record of being the tallest giant wheel in Europe. The London Eye can seat 800 people at once. In other words, the passengers on 11 London double-decker buses would fit on it!

Since the wheel opened to the public only in the year 2000, which is the millennium year, the London Eye is also called the Millennium Wheel. It was built "all over the world." While a team in the UK designed it, the wheel was constructed in the Netherlands using steel from the UK. The cables are Italian, and the bearings are German. Experts in the French Alps designed and developed the capsules, while the glass of the capsules was created in Venice. The car manufacturing giant, Skoda, also had a part to play in the building of the wheel. The spindle and hub of the London Eye were manufactured in Skoda's factory in the Czech Republic.

Interestingly, when first erected, the London Eye was only intended to be a temporary tourist attraction for five years. However, in 2002, the city authorities granted it a more permanent status, probably owing to its continued popularity among tourists. Even after standing tall for nearly 25 years, it continues to be the UK's most popular paid tourist attraction. Even celebrities can't stop being amazed by it. The supermodel Kate Moss has taken no less than 25 spins on it, while the American actor Jessica Alba has been on it 31 times!

When on the Eye, keep an eye out for:

- Buckingham Palace, Big Ben, and the Houses of Parliament, all of which should be visible, if it isn't cloudy.

- the sparking city lights, if you take a night trip.

- the 40-minute river cruise you can take from the London Eye on the Thames, taking you near St Paul's Cathedral, the Palace of Westminster, and many other prime locations.

Come now, detective, take out your magnifying glass and try to answer as many of the following as you can.

Fun and Trivia Questions

1. How many capsules does the London Eye have? How and why are they numbered so?

2. How long does one spin on the London Eye take?

3. What is special about the design of the London Eye? What makes it an architectural wonder?

4. What is the speed at which the London Eye turns?

5. What was one special capsule renamed in June 2013?

6. What is the weight of the London Eye?

7. What is special about its lighting? (Hint: It keeps changing, but according to what?)

Now, here are riddles to the bigger puzzle:

Riddles

One of the answers to the questions below is the greatest foe of the intruder.

- **Clue 3:** We are the one-eyed mascots of the 2012 London Olympics. Who are we?

- **Clue 4:** I have not just one, but eight to spare, so I'm not afraid of flying through the air on the London Eye. What am I?

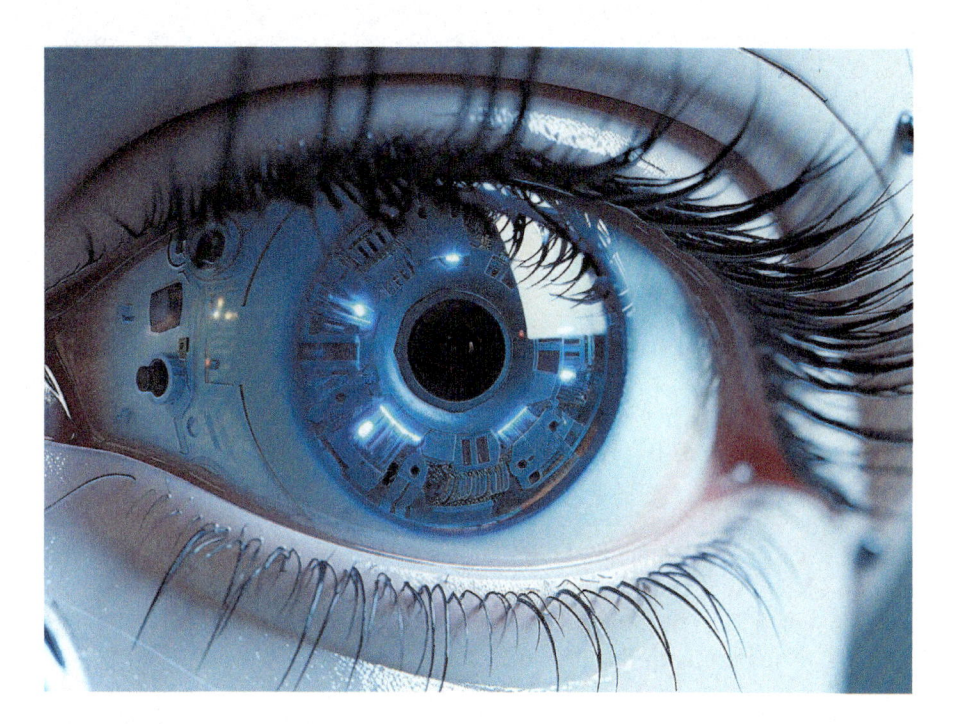

Onward now to our next location, travel detective!

15

Big Ben and the Houses of Parliament

Location: Palace of Westminster

Nearest Tube Station: ⬅️ 💂

Big Ben

You may well wonder why we seem to have two locations instead of one here. Let me clear up that confusion by telling you that Big Ben is a part of the Parliament buildings, which was originally the Palace of Westminster. But let us focus on this huge clock and its tower for a moment because no mention of London is ever complete without a reference to Big Ben, is it?

Interestingly, while most people still refer to the clock tower as Big Ben, the name was originally only for the Great Bell in the Great Clock of Westminster. There are two probable reasons for the naming of the Big Ben. One is that Sir Benjamin Hall, a Welsh civil engineer who was also a member of the House of Commons, was in charge of the bell's installation. The other reason was that there was a famous heavyweight boxer, Ben Caunt, known for bare-knuckle boxing in the 19th century.

The tower is not as old as the Westminster Palace. In fact, its construction was completed in 1859, during the reign of Queen Victoria. Perhaps you may not notice this in the photos or even videos of the tower, but it has elaborate stone carvings symbolizing all four nations of the UK—England, Wales, Scotland, and Northern Ireland. The tower is 316 ft high. The dials of each of the clocks have a diameter of 22.5 ft.

Despite being much more than 150 years old, the clock still uses the original mechanism from when it was made. It keeps such perfect time that it is usually not off by more than a second. However, there have been many incidents when the clock failed to chime or ran faster or slower than the actual time.

For four years, from 2017–2021, Big Ben never chimed, owing to the extensive repair work undertaken on the tower and the clocks. Though one of the dials was always visible to the public, the decision to mute the chimes was mainly so that the noise wouldn't hurt the ears of the workers employed on the renovations.

The Houses of Parliament: Palace of Westminster

The two houses of the UK Government, the House of Lords and the House of Commons, meet in buildings once part of the Westminster Palace. Today, "Westminster" refers to the parliament or the UK Government. So, if you were to read of "reports from Westminster," you should know that the reports are from the government or the parliament.

The original Westminster Palace was built during the times of King Edward the Confessor in the 11th Century. Some claim that there was a place on this site even before this! In 1512, the palace stopped being a royal residence when it was damaged by a fire. Parts of the palace were still used for parliament meetings. However, this too came to an end with another great fire in 1834.

The palace was then reconstructed for government use and reopened in 1860. Some parts of the original palace such as the Westminster Hall, Chapel of St Mary Undercroft, St Stephen's Cloister, and Jewel Tower were preserved and included in the buildings standing today. Do try to keep a look out for them if you have the chance!

Though the parliament buildings are not always open to the public, parts of the Westminster Palace, like Big Ben, are open to tourists. If you visit the houses, you will immediately know which house you are in by the color of the seats—green in the House of the Commons and red in the House of Lords. The House of Lords is open to the public, but you can enter and watch the chamber at work only after strict security measures like the ones we follow in airports.

Do you want to know more about the UK Parliament and Big Ben? Well, get cracking (make a move) on the following trivia questions, detective!

When you visit these two places, take special notice of:

- the Latin inscription under the clock face, which reads DOMINE SALVAM FAC REGINAM NOSTRAM VICTORIAM PRIMAM, which translates to "O Lord, keep safe our Queen Victoria the First."

- the special light above the clock faces, which is lit up only when the parliament is in session.

- The Jewel Tower, its ornate ceiling carvings, and the museum inside on the history of the British Parliament.

- the iconic statue of Boadicea and Her Daughters on Westminster Bridge on the crossing from Parliament Square. Boadicea was a queen of one of the native tribes of England who bravely fought but fell to the Romans.

- The number of bridges you can count if you take a river cruise from Westminster Pier.

Fun and Trivia Questions

1. How many faces does the Big Ben have? What colors are the clock and its hands?

2. How many steps would you have to climb to reach the top of the tower?

3. What is the tower housing Big Ben called?

4. What tune do the four smaller bells play every quarter hour?

5. Why do the doorkeepers of the House of Commons keep snuff boxes?

6. What was the famous Gunpowder Plot, and how was it related to the Parliament of England?

7. Why do the MPs and Peers of Parliament "vote with their feet"? (Hint: The answer to this might give you a back-to-school vibe.)

Hope you are not too knackered (tired), detective? Let us now proceed to the final two clues!

Riddles

Now the most awaited part of the chapter is here! Both the riddles below will help unmask the culprit at the Cabinet Office, beyond a shred of doubt.

- **Clue 5:** I'm a part of the Cabinet staff too, and I have been tasked with an important job. I am mostly in a hurry, furry, and keep some whiskered intruders away. I am related to one of the last two riddles you answered.

- **Clue 6, Answer to the Mystery:** The one above has been chasing us throughout, though we have given him the slip many times now. We are cousins to a creature you have already named in one of the five riddles above.

The Big Reveal

Congratulations and great job, travel detective! You have followed the clues and found the cheeky (shameless) intruder at 10 Downing Street and the Cabinet Office. Take some time to feel chuffed (overjoyed and proud) about your achievement.

A bigger adventure awaits you on the next leg of this journey.

Summary

- We covered three culturally important landmarks of London:

    - **Ministerial offices like the Cabinet Office and the prime minister's residence:** You learned the importance of 70 Whitehall and 10 Downing Street in the politics of the UK.

    - **The London Eye:** This Ferris Wheel has become a symbol of the London skyline and is one of the biggest tourist attractions. While riding it, you can see the entire city from the sky.

    - **Big Ben and the UK parliament:** If Big Ben is the most recognized structure of London, it is just as politically and culturally significant because it is a part of the Westminster Palace, where the Houses of Commons and Lords meet.

Next, let us proceed to the next set of locations in the big, colorful, and historic city of London. But wait, where exactly are we headed?

Here's a little clue: London's future is in jeopardy! Wizards, witches, and a stone, though not the Philosopher's Stone, will guide you ahead in your next adventure.

Safe journey super-sleuth!

CHAPTER 2:

Why Is the Future of London City in Jeopardy?

Introduction

Hey there, travel detective! Hope you are rested and ready for the adventures that await you in the next couple of destinations. But let's pause a while, and continue to learn a little more about what made London the city it is.

The City: Days of Yore

In the days of yore (a long time ago), London was not all glitz and glamor! Remember when we briefly mentioned the name "London" came from "Londinium," a city established by the Romans in the 1st century? Even before the Romans, England had native tribes, called the Celts or the Britons, who were driven away to other parts of the country by the invading Romans, who wanted the heart of fertile England.

Initially, ancient Romans occupied only a tiny part of the city, perhaps even as small as Hyde Park. However, they kept expanding the city, building it on the model of Roman cities, with public baths, temples, and an amphitheater, to meet the needs of the growing population. The Roman fort defended the city from invaders. Romans built the London Wall and six of the seven traditional gates that guarded London—Ludgate, Newgate, Aldersgate, Cripplegate, Bishopsgate, and Aldgate. Moorgate, alone, seems to have come later during the Middle Ages.

By the 5th century, as the Roman Empire in Europe weakened, the Romans left the kingdom open, and the Anglo-Saxon tribes of Western Europe invaded the country and slowly built their settlements. They plundered, looted, and torched down Roman architecture, but also developed and built on the remains and buildings left behind by the Romans. Though the Anglo-Saxons faced Viking and Scandinavian invasions in the 9th century and temporarily lost their control to the Viking kings, they eventually continued their rule till the French-Norman invasion of Britain in the 11th century.

Though the Norman invasion was, at first, marked by the use of the French language, practices, and customs, especially in the courts and offices of England, the native English and French cultures slowly began to mix. By the 14th century, which marked the end of the Middle Ages or the Medieval Era, there was, more or less, a single, unified British people.

"England" as we know it today is a mixture of native English, Roman, Anglo-Saxon, Viking, Norman, and several other influences. Amazing, isn't it?

Now, now, don't get all dull and depressed with this history lesson. I promise you some background information won't hurt you on the case to come.

Talking of which, here is a message explaining more about the mystery.

The Threat

Ahoy, travel detective!

London City is soon to be besieged by evil forces. Unravel the clues at each location below, until you can reveal the sinister plot at work! A lot of witchery and magic is at play, to say the least.

A note to the wise: Don't get too hooked up in all the spells, charms, and potions, lest you can't return to the game.

The Game is Afoot

Now, you know the safety of the city is at stake!

But before you begin, take a quick look at the rules of the game in the Introduction of Chapter 1.

All set, I hope? Ready, steady, go!

The Square Mile

Location: London City

There is a London City, sometimes simply referred to as "the City" or the "Square Mile" (because its area is just over one square mile) within Greater London. In other words, London Area includes London City and 32 other boroughs.

Is that too much to take in? Think of it this way:

London Area / Greater London = London City + 32 London boroughs.

To make the difference clearer, while the population of the whole of London is almost nine million, less than nine thousand have their gaffs (homes) in the City. Keep in mind, though, that 200,000 people travel to the City for work.

The Roman settlements and City Wall we discussed just a while ago were around this smaller London City. The City is where most of the financial and legal institutions of London are located—the Bank of England headquarters, the London Stock Exchange, The Temple or the buildings associated with the legal profession, and Guildhall, the London Corporation building. St. Paul's Cathedral is another one of the City's landmarks.

Let us now look at some interesting urban and cultural myths and facts about London that make it so unique. You can find out more such legends as you walk through the city.

- There is a myth that a bunch of wild Corgis, a breed of dogs, roam the city and attack people. These dogs are supposedly the offspring of Corgis abandoned by their owners in the 1980s. But this is likely to be a load of codswallop (stories made up for dramatic effect)!

- Another yarn goes that if Big Ben were to strike 13, the four huge bronze lions at the foot of Nelson's Column, Trafalgar Square, would come to life. Imagine the ruckus that would create in the city!

- The legend of Gogmagog and Corineus is equally shocking. It is said that the Roman Emperor Diocletian had 33 evil daughters, whom he thought to tame by marrying off. But, under the leadership of the eldest, Alba, these daughters murdered all their husbands. They were banished from Rome and set adrift on the sea in a boat. They arrived at an island full of demons. They named the island after the eldest sister, Albion. Gogmagog was one of the giants, who were the children of these princesses and the demons. Later, when the Roman Prince Aeneus came, he named the island "Britain". His warrior Corineus defeated Gogmagog. Even today during the Lord Mayor's Show in London, two huge figures made of wicker called either "Gog and Magog" or "Magog and Corineus" are carried around and considered guardians of the city. Albion was an ancient name for England, which you may come across in old stories, poems, or legends.

- Now, it's time for a not-so-daft (not-so-crazy) story. Hyde Park and Kensington Gardens have thousands of wild yellow and green parakeets. It is rumored that the iconic musician, Jimi Hendrix, while staying at Mayfair during the 1960s, released two rose-ringed parakeets, the same species that now inhabit the park. Since these birds do not migrate, it is thought that the London parakeets are descendants of Hendrix's pets.

- The City has several hidden churches, invisible from the street, built during the Middle Ages. Secret gardens also provide a place for rest and peace within the hustle and bustle of the City. There is also a network of tunnels connecting various parts of the Squaremile, which was built for storage, defence, or transportation. Of course, the tunnels aren't open to the public, but just knowing they exist should make you feel gobsmacked (very surprised).

So, detective, are you full of beans (full of energy)? Let's move on to the fun questions!

Fun and Trivia Questions

1. Which famous London City park has an old pet cemetery, sometimes called haunted?

2. What are the "flying rats" you can't feed on Trafalgar Square?

3. What color are London's official taxi cabs? Why are they called "hackney carriages"?

4. What's the name of the imaginary English nanny created by writer P. L. Travers? (Hint: She arrives on a rainbow, holding an umbrella at the Banks family home, 17 Cherry Tree Lane.)

5. Which London airport is the busiest in the UK and transports more than 80 million passengers in a typical year? (Hint: It even has a "ghost station" under it.)

6. This is the oldest transportation system of its kind in the world, and it opened in 1863 in London. By 1890, it became electrified. What are we talking about?

7. What are the "fake houses" near Hyde Park?

Are you ready to rack your brains to unravel the clues to the threat that looms over London? Here goes!

Riddles

<u>One of the clues</u> below will point you to the location of the possible threat to the city.

- **Clue 1:** Heavy and dark, with an open mouth, in battles long ago I was used to fire at enemies. In my name is a famous street that houses an ancient secret.

- **Clue 2:** I go from corner to corner in squares. In my name is hidden a place where witches and wizards buy their school supplies.

- **Clue 3:** I knead the dough and work the yeast. In the oven, my creations are fit for a feast—pies, pastries, and bread. A street in my name is home to a famous detective like you. Who am I?

And so let us proceed to our next location on the trail of more clues.

The Studio of Magic

Location: Leavesden, Watford

Nearest Railway Station: 💧 − er + ford Junction

Hope you are not too zonked out (exhausted) with all that investigating. This next location will thrill your very soul. You'll shortly arrive at the Warner Bros Studios Tour London, which will give you an inside glimpse into the heart of Hogwarts itself. You will visit the Harry Potter film sets and be privy to many wondrous secrets.

There is an interesting history associated with this place. Originally an airfield in Leavesden in Watford, this land was once owned by de Havilland Aircraft Company and the British Air Ministry. The Leavesden Aerodrome carried out the important task of producing airplanes during WWII. After the war, de Havilland sold the land to Rolls Royce, the famous car manufacturing company. However, over time, the airfield was abandoned and forgotten, until it was rediscovered and first used as a film set for the 1994 James Bond movie, *GoldenEye*. In 1999, the open spaces and hangars of the airfield were found to be perfect for the filming of *Harry Potter*. The rest is history. Warner Bros bought the studio in 2010 and opened it to the public in 2012.

Here are some things you should not miss at any cost!

- You can walk through the actual sets of the Hogwarts Dining Hall, the Forbidden Forest, Gringotts Wizarding Bank, and Diagon Alley. You can even take a ride on the Hogwarts Express!

- You will see some of the original costumes and props the actors used during the shooting. The guided tour also includes an experience of the animation and sound effects used in the movies.

- If you are sure you won't leg it (run away) in fright, you can also see life-size replicas of creatures from the movies such as the Basilisk, Hippogriff, the giant spider (Aragog), and the goblins at Gringotts Bank.

- This guided tour of all the major sets used for the *Harry Potter* movies takes at least three and a half hours to complete. So, be prepared to walk lots and marvel even more.

So, detective, are you buzzin' (excited) for more? Let's get on with the trivia questions.

Fun and Trivia Questions

1. We know J. K. Rowling wrote *Harry Potter*, but where did she get the inspiration for the main character's name?

2. Did you know that the opening of the Studio Tours was attended by some members of the royal family? Who were they?

3. How many visitors can the London Warner Bros Studio Tours accommodate in one day?

4. What is the prop in the Great Hall that is rumored to have caused a national shortage of Indian glass beads when it was built?

5. How large is the Ministry of Magic set?

6. In the *Harry Potter* books, what is the word used to refer to people without magical abilities?

Come, come, travel detective, no time to stand around faffing (doing nothing or idling away time)! It is riddle time now!

Riddles

One of the stones below is linked to the safety of London. Hasten now to identify which is the right stone and which is the red herring.

- **Clue 4:** On the Isle of Grain, beside Yantlet Creek, I stand. Forgotten and old, I used to mark the limits of London city.

- **Clue 5:** In London's heart, on a street you have already named, I stand with pride. Centuries-old, secrets inside, witness to the city's history.

All right then, let's get moving to the final destination of this chapter and hopefully wind up the mystery before it's too late!

The Stone of Brutus: The Heart of London

Location: 111, Cannon Street

Nearest Tube Station: 💣 🛣️

In an often-overlooked and forgotten corner of London City is a stone, which has several legends and stories associated with it. All that you can see of it now is a block of limestone, inside a wall with a glass front. The London Stone, located on Cannon Street, is the stone in question.

Some people consider it an altar the Druidic priests of the Anglo-Saxon era set up or a Roman milestone used to mark distances from the city center to other places. It has also been claimed to be a part of the altar that the Roman Brutus of Troy built when he founded London in 1000 B.CE. Now, it is called the "heart of London," it is one of the most ancient landmarks of the city, and it has hardly been moved from its original location for centuries together. It shows up on maps of the city from the 16th century onwards.

Originally, the stone was always located on Cannon Street, though the street was renamed as that only later. As with other buildings, the London Stone was also partially damaged by the Great Fire of 1666. What we see today is only a part of the original London Stone. By 1720, the stone was moved into a small, stone cupola to protect it. It was moved around a bit in the 17th and 18th centuries until it found its place in the wall of the Wren Church of St Swithin for a hundred years.

The church was destroyed in the bombing of London during World War II, and the stone was removed to the Guildhall Museum. The present location of the stone was established in 1962, only at the time, it was a grilled alcove instead of the one with the glass cover. In 2016, the stone was briefly moved to the London Museum while the new recess with the glass cover was prepared, and then the stone was moved back to Cannon Street in 2018.

One of the more popular legends associated with the stone is that of Jack Cade, leader of the Kentish rebellion against the corrupt rule of King Henry VI, who in 1450 entered the city, struck London Stone with his sword, and proclaimed it to be "lord of this city."

When you visit the stone, ensure you:

- take photos of it and gather as many stories about it as possible!

- visit the Monument to the Great Fire of London, walkable from Cannon Street. It is a single Doric column built between 1671 and 1677, standing not far from Pudding Lane where the fire started. This monument also has panoramic cameras on its top, providing detailed information about weather and other activity around the area.

- take a guided tour of the Mansion House, Walbrook, which is less than three minutes away by walk. It is home to the Lord Mayor of London, an 18th-century building, and even houses the rare Harold Samuel Collection of 17th-century Dutch and Flemish paintings.

Enough with the history lessons, detective. It is time to move on to the trivia questions.

Fun and Trivia Questions

1. How big is the London Stone?

2. What was Cannon Street originally called, and where did that name come from?

3. Why was the London Stone moved from where it was located in the middle of the street to the curbside?

4. Who is claimed to have chipped off pieces of the stone in the 16th century, and why?

5. What is the relationship between London Stone and the mythical and famous King Arthur of England?

6. The plaque placed next to the London Stone says that its original purpose was _____.

    A. unknown   b. part of Roman buildings   c. an altar

If you have successfully answered the above, it's time to reveal the big secret at last. Find out how London's future is in jeopardy by solving this last question below.

Riddle

Answer the riddle below and voila! You have the mystery in this chapter solved!

Clue 6, Answer to the Mystery: A simple relation there is between London's future and the Stone. The Stone is the "Palladium" of the city. Find what the Palladium was, and all will reveal itself.

The Big Reveal

Congratulations, travel detective. You have again successfully followed each and every clue and discovered how the future of the city can be saved in one small action (or should I say inaction?)

There is still more of London yet to be explored, so tarry not, but let's get moving.

Summary

- The three fascinating places that we covered in this section include:
    - **The City:** This is the City within the city, or the original Londinium that the Romans established. This is a small area around one square mile, from which it gets its name The Square Mile.
    - **The Warner Bros Studio Tours, London:** We completed an amazing exploration of the sets where the *Harry Potter* movies were breathed into life. From props, special effects, and sets that were used for the movie, you can revisit every single detail here.
    - **The London Stone:** Located on Cannon Street is the Heart of the City, and it is as old as the city itself. Simply understanding the myths that surround this unassuming block of stone should give you goosebumps because it will transport you to a long-gone era.

Let's proceed to more well-known tourist spots in the city. Here is a little something to give you a hint of what is coming next.

The city's law, religion, and recreation play a part in the next adventure to save a few lives.

CHAPTER 3:

The Mystery of the Trapped Tourists

Introduction

How has this journey turned out for you, travel detective? You should be extremely proud of how far you have come. There is still lots more in store for you. But, before we jump into traveling and solving crimes, let us quickly introduce you to the city some more. This time, let us focus on information we haven't already covered.

The City: Greenery and Nature

London continues to be so many different things that it can be hard to pin down a single trait of the city. As one of the first industrial capitals of the world, London was filled with so much smoke and pollution that residents once called it "The Big Smoke." The word "smog," a combination of smoke and fog, was coined to describe it. Londoners also called these smogs "pea soupers" because of their thick and yellowy appearance, resembling, you guessed it, the pea soup!

However, you will be surprised to know that by the United Nations' definition, London is one of the world's largest urban forests. This is because it has (Wood, 2019 & Mata, 2023):

- more than 0.5 hectares in area.

- trees that are taller than 5 meters. The UK government website tells us that London has 8.4 million trees in private and public spaces.

- a canopy cover of more than 10% of London's area. A canopy is the leafy ceiling or roof that trees offer us.

Isn't it great that for less than 9 million people in the city, there are over 8 million trees?

We know London lies across the River Thames. However, what we did not say is that many other big and small rivers drain into the Thames. The city also has at least 12 rivers running underground, hidden from plain sight! Some of these rivers once ran above the ground but were closed down for construction or other reasons. For instance, the River Fleet became so polluted by local butchers throwing meat into it that it was finally converted into a sewer. The Oval cricket stadium was built partly using the mud dug out from the closing of River Effra. River Tyburn, which now flows under Buckingham Palace, with only a small part of it visible in Regent's Park, was once a fine fishing spot for salmon. Despite these "lost" rivers, London still has many canals, originally constructed for the transportation of goods but now only used for boating and picnics.

Though mainly flat, London has small hills such as Ludgate Hill, Crown Hill, Corn Hill, Primrose Hill, Shooter's Hill, Tower Hill, and plenty more for those who love trekking or walking. Probably the most famous one, because of the 1999 movie of the same name, is Notting Hill. Some of these hills and surrounding areas also have beautiful parks for people to stroll in.

London has a pleasant climate with showers all through the year. In summer, the days are about 18°C, while in winter, although it snows only for a day or two, it gets as cold as 4°C (Clout et al., 2024). To give you an idea of how hot or cold that is, our bodies are generally 37°C, and water freezes into ice at 0°C. And don't be fooled by the Londoner's constant grumbles about the rain. Though London does receive a fair bit of rainfall, you can easily expect many dry days in the city too. So, maybe you can put away that brolly and anorak (umbrella and raincoat) today!

Well, we have run on quite a bit about the city's weather and nature. Let's get down to business, travel detective, shall we?

Oh, look, just in time too! Is that a message from the City Police?

The Problem

Good morning, travel detective. We have a problem. We got an anonymous tip-off about tourists trapped somewhere in the city. We don't know the exact location. Meet us down at the Met. Chop chop (hurry)!

Buckle Up!

Well, here we go, detective. The Met is the Metropolitan Police Department, so it seems you have a big case this time!

But before you begin, be sure to keep in mind the rules of the game in the Introduction of Chapter 1 again!

Are you rearing to go? Ready, steady, go!

Scotland Yard

Location: Victoria Embankment, Westminster

Nearest Tube Station: ⬅️ 💂

The headquarters and the police force of the London Metropolitan Police have always been called "Scotland Yard," a reference to their first office in the city, 4 Whitehall Place, in 1829, which had a public entrance into the Great Scotland Yard Street. Scotland Yard was called so because it used to have a palace where Scottish royalty stayed when visiting the city. Of course, by the time the police headquarters was established the palace was long gone. Interestingly, this first office is open to the public as a five-star luxury hotel by Hyatt and is called the Great Scotland Yard Hotel today.

Since the first headquarters was established, the London Police headquarters moved three times to accommodate the growing size of the force. By 1890, a brand new building was constructed on Victoria Embankment, in what became known as the "New Scotland Yard." By the 1940s, this building itself grew into a three-building complex for the police. These buildings are now protected heritage sites of the city and called the Norman Shaw buildings.

In 1967, another building was constructed on Broadway, where the headquarters and staff were again moved. The Broadway building was eventually sold off and demolished.

Finally, in 2015, the present building was constructed on the Victoria Embankment, moving the force nearer back to the Norman Shaw Buildings. Wherever the force moves, it seems to carry along the tag of "New Scotland Yard." Scotland Yard cannot be separated from London's past, present, or future. Many famous books, movies, and crimes set in the city reference the force by that particular name.

If you go near any of the old Scotland Yard buildings:

- Try to get yourself into a walking tour such as London's Great Scotland Yard Private Tour, which will give you an idea of Scotland Yard's place in English history.

Now, detective, don't get all miffed (confused and annoyed) at all this shifting around. Let's just get on with the fun questions!

Fun and Trivia Questions

1. Can you name two famous fictional detectives who worked hand-in-glove with the Scotland Yard? (Clues: They were created by Arthur Conan Doyle and Agatha Christie).

2. What is the name of the private museum at the Scotland Yard? What is it famous for?

3. What modern forensic practice was promoted by Scotland Yard? (Hint: It is one of the main reasons they say you should not touch anything in a crime scene.)

4. What percentage of patrol officers in London carry guns today, 10% or 50%? (This may come as a huge surprise!)

5. Who are Scotland Yard's "Super Recognizers"? (Hint: They can do even better than CCTV!)

Alright detective, is something looking a bit dodgy (fishy)? Let's move on to the questions that could bring you closer to where the tourists could be!

Riddles

Solve the clues below to find more. One of the following secret gardens is our next location, while the other is a beautiful spot to explore when you have time on your hands.

- **Clue 1:** My grounds contain a 1,000-year-old secret garden where the monks of yore used to grow their food. This is the oldest garden in England under continuous cultivation. What building am I?

- **Clue 2:** I was an ancient shrine, destroyed partly by the Great Fire and then almost completely by bombing in the Second World War. In my ruins a garden lies, easily missed, if you don't search for it.

And now, if all the investigating hasn't knocked your socks off (amazed you), let's move to the next place. Prepare to be charmed by the beauty of one of London's most famous churches.

Britain's Valhalla

Location: Dean's Yard, Westminster

Nearest Tube Station: 👼 🧃 es 🏔️

London is predominantly Christian, with 46% of the population being Christians. The next biggest section of the population, around 37%, doesn't identify with or believe in any religion. Other religions in the city include Muslims, Hindus, Jews, Sikhs, Buddhists, and others (ONS, 2021).

London has about 50 churches. Not all of these churches belong to the same Christian sects, though. Since the 16th century, the Church of England has been the official church of the country. The Westminster Abbey, formally called the Collegiate Church of Saint Peter at Westminster, is one of the most important churches as it is where all the kings and queens of England have been crowned since the church was built in 1066. Many of the monarchs also have their final resting places in the Abbey. The Abbey has seen several royal marriages and baptisms as well.

Do not confuse Westminster Abbey with the Westminster Cathedral, which is Catholic and comes under the Pope in the Vatican. There are other protestant churches, which work independently of the Anglican church in London. For instance, the Westminster Chapel is an evangelical free church.

Westminster Abbey is historically significant because it was built by the Anglo-Saxon King, Edward the Confessor in the 11th century. He is buried in the church as well. Later, in the 13th and 14th centuries, the church got its Gothic facelift. Some parts of the earlier church were demolished and rebuilt too. Though much of the medieval structure is still intact, the Westminster Abbey saw major renovations and some additions in the 18th century. The Northern entrance of the church has three porches, one of which has a beautifully carved semicircular arch. This has earned the Northern entrance the title "Solomon's Porch," a reference to the Biblical temple King Solomon built in Jerusalem.

An interesting part of the church is the Poet's Corner, where great English philosophers, poets, actors, thinkers, scientists, artists, and others have been buried or have had memorials erected in their names. Some of the most famous people whose tombs you can see include Sir Isaac Newton, Charles Dickens, Charles Darwin, and Stephen Hawkins. In Norse myths, Valhalla is the final resting place of selected warrior heroes. This is why the abbey is sometimes nicknamed "Britain's Valhalla".

Keep your eyes peeled at Westminster Abbey for:

- Tomb of the Unknown Warrior, the resting place of an unnamed hero killed in action on the western front during WWI. This honors all the unnamed soldiers who died in the war

- Poet's Corner and the people resting or commemorated there

- Coronation Chair of the kings and queens

- the royal tombs including that of Edward the Confessor

- Lady Chapel, with the resting places of queens and kings and its magnificent architecture.

If you have soaked in all that history, let us go straight to the trivia!

Fun and Trivia Questions

1. Why is the Westminster Abbey part of the "Royal Peculiar"? (What is so peculiar about the Abbey?)

2. How many people are buried here?

3. Which is the oldest door in England?

4. What is the height of the Abbey's ceiling?

5. What is the Cosmati Pavement, where is it, and what does it predict?

6. What was the famous stone stolen from the Abbey? (Hint: It reminds you of buttery scones).

Let's hope your mouth is now watering for a taste of the big mystery, detective! Here goes!

Riddles

One of the theaters below is near the next location we will visit, while the other is nearer still to where the trapped tourists are. Find which is which, quick!

- **Clue 3:** My name should remind you of a monument, the largest of its kind built in ancient Rome.

- **Clue 4:** I am a theater more ancient still, which has been rebuilt four times in all. I sit on London's oldest theater site.

And now, detective, let us visit the last location, and hopefully, you should be able to solve the puzzle once and for all.

The Garden of the Abbey and Convent

Covent Garden is an area of London between the West End and the central city. It is basically a large market square, which is a shopper's delight. For over 300 years, it hosted London's biggest fruit, flower, and vegetable markets. In fact, some historians claim that even the Anglo-Saxons had trading posts in Covent Garden.

39

There is an interesting history behind the name of the place. When Westminster Abbey was under the Benedictine Monks, they had a "convent garden" where they grew all manner of produce herbs, plants, vegetables, and fruits. Over time, The Garden of the Abbey and Convent became "Covent Garden."

When King Henry VIII decided to capture the churches of England, Covent Garden became the property of the crown rather than that of the church. It was one of the later aristocrats, the Earl of Bedford, who decided to not just build a house for himself on the north side but also develop the area into a piazza or square with many houses. The Earl also asked the royal architect who was commissioned for the project, Inigo Jones, to build a church, "not better than a barn" because he did not want to shell out more money than was necessary. St. Paul's Church, "the handsomest barn in London" according to Inigo Jones, was thus built.

With the piazza and church in place, it was only a matter of time before sellers arrived at Covent Garden and put up open markets. The initial temporary stalls were replaced with a more permanent system when King Charles II granted the markets permission to be held every day except Sundays and Christmas Day.

Very soon, other meeting and entertainment hubs sprang up around the area, including pubs, taverns, gambling houses, theaters, coffee houses, and bookshops. The market areas were also given facelifts over the years. Upper stories of shops enabled people of the upper classes to shop in peace without having to mingle with the crowds (Tucker, 2024).

Even today Covent Garden is the bee's knees (the best of its kind) where touristy things are concerned. You can:

- visit the many museums around here.
- watch a performance at the theater and opera houses, which provide world-class entertainment.
- visit and take selfies at the Infinity Chamber, lit up by hundreds of LED lights.
- sample the food and shopping centers the place is flooded with.

So, detective, on to the trivia then. With your increasing experience, you should be able to answer these questions like Bob's your uncle (easily or without much trouble)!

Fun and Trivia Questions

1. Why is Covent Garden called the first piazza in London?
2. What supernatural stories are associated with Theater Royal and the Royal Opera House in Covent Garden?
3. Which is the oldest pub in Covent Garden, and what is its nickname?
4. What now-famous street show involving two puppets can you see in Covent Garden?
5. What fruit represented Covent Garden, and why? (Hint: 🪴 + 🍎)
6. Why is Covent Garden considered the birthplace of the sandwich?

7. The Cockney dialect of London, or the English originally spoken by the working classes, is interesting for its unique pronunciation and words. Eliza Doolittle, the Covent Garden flower girl from George Bernand Shaw's play *Pygmalion*, which became the classic musical *My Fair Lady* (1964), speaks this dialect. What does "apples and pears" in Cockney slang mean in common English?

Hey, detective, hope your brain is not chockablock (full to the brim) with information. Hope you have some space in your head to solve the puzzle of the tourists! Here is the final riddle.

Riddles

And finally, we have the answer to the mystery in this chapter, one final clue away:

Clue 5, Answer to the Mystery: A narrow alley, I connect St Martin's Lane and Bedfordbury. I run along the walls of one of the theaters you have already named. Find me on the map and you will find the poor trapped tourists.

The Big Reveal

Hearty congratulations, dear travel detective, you have done it yet again! Because of your quick wits, the tourists have been saved. In all this while, you have made not a single clanger (blunder or mistake). Keep up the work!

It's now time to go off gallivanting (roaming on an adventure) again!

Summary

We visited three interesting places just now:

- **Scotland Yard:** This is the headquarters of London's police force, and the term is also used to refer to the force itself. The buildings the police occupy may have changed, but their commitment to providing law and order in the city has not.

- **Westminster Abbey:** This place is historically important for the whole of UK because it is the church where royal coronations have happened since the 11th century. With the right blend of history and beauty, this old church is a symbol of the UK's future too.

- **Covent Garden:** From the convent kitchen gardens, this location has come a long way in becoming one of London's top tourist spots. It is where you can hope to shop to your heart's content while soaking in the culture and history of this famous city.

As we move ahead, a little teaser will keep you guessing about our next adventure: Get prepared to save the Crown Jewels and perhaps the future of the monarchy itself!

Brace yourself, travel detective! Here we go!

CHAPTER 4:

The Mystery of Saving the British Monarchy

Introduction

Hope you are all geared up for this next mystery. As usual though, let us ease into the case with some more information about London city. This time, let us focus a little on London's economy and how it has strengthened over time.

The City: Coins and Cash

Colloquially, the English refer to money as "quid." Since money is an essential aspect of a city, let us quickly look at how London has become so powerful.

The Industrial Revolution started in Great Britain in the 18th century and soon spread to other countries in Europe and North America. It saw the setting up of huge factories and the widespread mechanization of processes, which had all been done by hand till then. With the rapid progress of technology, mass production of things became possible. Some important innovations of the time were power looms and cotton gins used in the textile industry, steam engines used in industries, more efficient and better production of iron, and the invention of machine tools. Almost every industry, including agriculture, textile, transportation, paper making, and glass manufacturing, suddenly grew. All this helped cities like Manchester and London grow.

Of course, there has been a shift in London's economy. Whereas agriculture and the production of goods were once in demand, today, areas such as the service industries are growing. Industries doing great in London include management services, computer technology, sports, real estate, security and investigation services, and architecture and engineering. Over the years, London has also become one of the most favored places for international investors. Some of the world's richest people stay in London.

26% of the people working in London are non-UK citizens. In other words, people from all over the world want to work in London, adding to its diversity and skilled workforce. From 1990 to 2020, London saw an increase in jobs from 3.8 million to 5.3 million (Whitehead et al., 2020).

If all that doesn't say a lot about the development of a city, what does?

Well, detective, perhaps you are thinking that the lecture is getting a little too dull for your taste. Don't fret, news about the mystery is already headed your way.

The Case

Oh, travel detective! This time we seem to have a curious case at hand. There is a threat to the monarchy, and only you can save the king from harm. May the ravens (yes, the birds) guide you.

Let It Roll!

Looks like the king and his court are in trouble!

But before you dive into action, quickly remind yourself of the rules of the game from the Introduction to Chapter 1 again.

So, full steam ahead! Ready, steady, go!

The East End and Whitechapel

Perhaps you recognize London's East End from the popular BBC series *East Enders* or have seen it in iconic movies like *Bridget Jones' Diary* (2001) or *Lock, Stock and Two Smoking Barrels* (1998). This part of London has its own flavor and way of life, quite different from the Western and central parts of the city. Let us look at what makes East End tick and what you could enjoy seeing and experiencing here.

A unique aspect of the eastern part of the city is that it was always inhabited by the poorer and working sections of the population. In fact, East End is also where a majority of the people from poor countries in the world immigrated. For instance, East End has Brick Lane, where many Bangladeshi textile industry workers lived in cramped quarters. Similarly, it is also a place where many of the poorer Jewish people worked and lived. Culturally diverse, the East End has many languages spoken and religions practiced.

Frustrations related to poverty, unemployment, and lack of resources may be why there is a higher rate of crime and violence in the East End as compared to other parts of the city. One of the most (in)famous personalities of East End is Jack the Ripper, the late 19th-century serial killer who brutally killed at least five women around the Whitechapel area. There were probably more victims, but no proof clearly links him to some of the other murders. He was also called the "Whitechapel Murderer" or "Leather Apron" because many women around the area mentioned a man who habitually wore a leather apron and scared them. It was also suspected he wore a leather apron while brutally cutting up his victims so that the blood would not splatter on him. People the world over continue to be fascinated with his identity as he was never officially caught.

Interestingly, the name "Whitechapel" came from the nearby church of St Mary Matfelon, which was whitewashed to make it look clean and respectable. Whitechapel, Shoreditch, Holborn, and other nearby areas were the center for the more polluting industries of London such as tanneries where leather is made, laundry and clothes dyers, soap manufacturers, butchers, and breweries where alcohol is made. This, and the fact that most workers were poor, often made these areas crowded and dirty.

Whitechapel also had famous foundries such as the Whitechapel Bell Foundry, which opened in 1570, where Big Ben and other famous bells such as the Liberty Bell of Philadelphia and the Bow Bells of the Church of St Mary-le-Bow at Cheapside were cast. Until its shutdown in 2016, it was considered the oldest manufacturing company in the UK.

Today, of course, Whitechapel has its own art and other tourist attractions.

Things to do when you are in the East End include:

- a visit to the Ripper Museum located in Cable Street, which has an assortment of objects, reports, and photos related to the victims and suspects in the Jack the Ripper case.

- a tour of the Whitechapel Art Gallery, established in 1901, where works of various artists are exhibited temporarily.
- a look at the mural paintings around the area, depicting famous people, events, incidents, and other political, historical, and artistic ideas that have affected and shaped Whitechapel's identity.

Enough with all the chinwag (gossip). It's that time again, innit (isn't it)? It's time for the fun and trivia questions, guaranteed to make you a super sleuth.

Fun and Trivia Questions

1. In Charles Dickens's famous children's book *Oliver Twist,* an old man trains young boys like the Artful Dodger and Charley Bates to become pickpockets He also has a den in Saffron Hill, Holborn. Is this evil character Fagin or Monks?

2. What is the present name of the park that housed the St Mary Matfelon church that gave Whitechapel its name? Why was it renamed?

3. Which is the luxury dept store, located now in Brompton Road, Knightsbridge, that had its humble origins in the East End?

4. Can you find Aldgate now? Why? How did it get its name?

5. What famous sculpture from the Roman period did archaeologists find in Aldgate in 2013? Was it the Minories Eagle or the Statue of Trajan?

6. The Royal London Hospital in Whitechapel has a museum dedicated to a man. Who was he?

7. If somebody asks you in the Cockney slang whether you fancy a "Ruby Murray" tonight, what are they talking about?

Well, now for the canny (nice) mystery of this episode. The riddles await you, mate (friend)!

Riddles

The clues below will provide more information on our next locations detectives.

- **Clue 1:** A famous hospital still, I was first located just outside the city walls. I gained a fearsome reputation, and many horror and thriller stories are set inside me. Who am I, and how am I related to the wall?

- **Clue 2:** A famous garden and square today, I was built on the site where hundreds, out of favor with the crown, lost their lives. I have something to do with the number three, too.

Travel detective, time to move on to the final location of this adventure!

The Wall and Tower Hill

Nearest Tube Station:

The London Wall was one of the biggest projects the Romans carried out in the city. Built between 190 and 250 AD and defining the very shape of London, it is no wonder we give the wall such importance. When the Romans built it, its length was 4 km, or 13,123 ft, and it enclosed around 330 acres of land. The Hollywood Walk of Fame is only a little more than half this length at 2.5 km. The wall also had gates letting people in and out of the city. Today, the wall is not continuous, and you can only see sections of it standing here and there.

The Romans put a lot of effort into building the wall. They transported huge quantities of Kentish ragstone by Thames and Medway to build it. It was built to a height of 6 meters or 19 feet, though there could have been sections of the wall that were taller than this.

After the Romans left, the Anglo-Saxons repaired parts of the wall that had been damaged and used it for the same purpose—to defend the city. By the Middle Ages, the wall was raised to a height of 10 m, or 32 ft, and additional gates were added. During that time, the city officials would ring a bell to let the citizens know when it was time to close the gates in the evening. Anyone found wandering after curfew was rung was imprisoned unless they could produce a valid reason for being out on the streets.

Today, the street running beside the wall is also called the London Wall. Some parts of the wall are underground. In 1987-88, digging revealed about 100 ft or 30 m of the wall underneath the earth at the American Square. When the Romans lived in London, burying the dead within city limits was banned. They built two large graveyards outside Bishopsgate in Spitalfields, which were only discovered in the 15th century. The graveyards were torn down and used for construction in the 18th century (CityDays, 2023 & *History of London Wall,* n.d.)

The area surrounding the Tower of London in the Borough of Tower Hamlets is the Tower Hills. Historically, it had scaffolds for public executions, where criminals and other people who were unpopular or disliked by the Crown were beheaded. Over 120 executions have been recorded to have happened here. Tower Hill starts from the North Bank of the River Thames and reaches a maximum height of 14.5 m or 48 ft. Most of the hill area continues to be open lands because city authorities have always wanted to make sure that buildings on it don't obstruct the view of the Tower of London.

As you visit these parts:

- Take part in one of the numerous Roman Wall Walks around the city, which will give you a history of the place.
- Visit 10 Trinity Square, Tower Hill, which was once the headquarters of the Port of London Authority and is now a restaurant and hotel. It preserves the original interiors of the building from the 1920s.

Well, let's stop right there and you, travel detective, can have a go at the questions now.

Fun and Trivia Questions

1. How can you understand whether a place in London was within or outside the wall in olden times?
2. Where were parts of the London Wall discovered opposite the Museum of London?
3. This hall tower was built in the 13th century, damaged in the Great Fire, rebuilt, but again damaged in WWII. What is this hall tower, the remains of which you can still see?
4. Which church has its vestry built into the foundations of the London Wall bastion?
5. Which of the gates rebuilt in the Middle Ages was where the newly executed prisoners' heads were displayed on the spikes?
6. This part of the London Wall was found in a subway during excavations in 1977. Where is this?
7. Over which London City gate lived one of the most important English writers, who was called the "Father of English Poetry"?

Now, if your head's not reeling too much, let's move on to how the monarchy may be in danger with the riddles below.

Riddles

Solve the clues below, detective. One of them will take you to the final destination of this adventure, and one is a red herring.

- **Clue 3:** I have been a palace, zoo, prison, and fortress. Now, I hold jewels of the kingdom. Who am I, and what do I hold?
- **Clue 4:** I am a bridge in a nursery rhyme, always said to be collapsing. Who am I?

The Bridge and the Royal Fortress

Location: London Borough of Tower Hamlets

Nearest Tube Station: 🏰 🌅

Though it may seem that the Tower Bridge is an extension of the nearby London Tower, it is much newer than you would think. The Tower Bridge was constructed in 1894, and its design was selected from 50 entries submitted as part of a competition. This makes the bridge only 130 years old. However, it was built in the Gothic style of architecture so it would match the London Tower.

The bridge is 800 ft or 240 m long and 200 ft or 61 m high. However, that's when the drawbridge is closed. The Tower Bridge has two sections in the central span, called bascules or leaves, that can be raised up to an angle of 83 degrees. Each of the bascules weigh a whopping 1,100 tons! Since there is no longer as much activity in the London Docklands, the bascules are not often raised now. In fact, a popular myth goes that seeing the bascules opening will bring the onlooker luck! In 1952, a rather curious thing happened. A bus was on the bridge when the leaves of the bridge started to open. Instead of slamming the brakes, the driver, Albert Gunton, accelerated and the bus jumped from the south to the north bascule. Luckily, the north bascule hadn't started rising and nobody was hurt. There have also been instances of a small plane and a jet that flew between the walkway and the bascules of the bridge! Blimey (an exclamation of surprise), indeed!

The Tower of London has, at various times in history, been a royal zoo, fortress, palace, and prison. It was built as a fort in the second century during the reign of King William I the Conqueror. In the 12th and 13th centuries, the fort was further extended, with the original White Tower of the building becoming a central point around which other layers of fortifications were built. There are many towers around the White Tower such as the Bloody Tower, Wakefield Tower, and Beauchamp Tower.

The Tower of London also had a moat around it. It was built more as a defensive ditch by William I. In the 1240s, under King Henry III, this ditch was converted into a moat that surrounded the entire tower. By the 1270s, the moat was further deepened and was pretty much the same shape as we see it today. It was about 50 ft wide. Edward I filled the moat with pike, and it was a great spot for fishing enthusiasts of the day. However, a century later, in the 1840s, an epidemic spread, and the moat smelled so foul that it had to be drained and cleaned. Since then, the moat has always remained dry.

The land of the moat was, however, put to good use by the staff and people around. It was often used as a patch of land to grow vegetables and fruits. Cattle grazed on the land ,keeping weeds and grass in check. During WWII, people were allotted lands including the moat area to grow produce to help with the rationing and food shortage during the period.

Things to do and look out for during your visit to the Tower Bridge and Tower of London are:

- Stroll on the walkway between the two towers of the bridge, which though originally built in steel and concrete as a way for pedestrians to cross when the bascules were open, was rebuilt in glass in 2014. You can take in the sights over the Thames.

- Sight the steam-driven hydraulic pumps operating the Tower Bridge. Though these pumps were replaced by electric motors in 1976, the pumps are still in working condition!

- Keep your eyes peeled for the crown jewels in the Tower of London. Till 1994, it was displayed in an underground chamber of the Tower, while a more convenient room above the ground is used today.

- Engage in the Gunpowder Plot Immersive Experience in the Tower Vaults at the Tower of London, where stunning stage settings, sounds, special effects, live actors, and digital actors like Tom Felton of *Harry Potter* fame will make you a part of the secret plot of 1605.

Let us now fly to the questions and trivia and then to the riddles that should solve the case pronto!

Fun and Trivia Questions

1. The Tower Bridge is often mistaken for another bridge that has a nursery rhyme about it. What is this rhyme, and what does it mean?

2. What is the Ceremony of Keys that has taken place over 700 years at the Tower of London?

3. What do the Crown Jewels mainly include apart from two scepters, an orb, an ampulla, a pair of spurs, a pair of armills or bracelets, and a staff?

4. Why are the Yeoman Warders of the Tower of London also called Beefeaters?

5. What color is the Tower Bridge today? What is the history behind this?

6. The male heir to the British throne is traditionally given which title?

    A. Prince of Wessex b. Prince of Sussex c. Prince of Wales d. Prince of York

And now, ready or not, detective, let us head to the final riddle!

Riddles

Solve me and you will have solved the mystery in this chapter!

Clue 5, Answer to the Mystery: We are six. Winged, dark, and intelligent, we have been feared as bringers of bad luck. We occupy the Tower and ensure the Kingdom is safe. Who are we, and how do we protect the kingdom?

The Big Reveal

A big congrats to you, if you have got this far. And four mysteries solved is no mean feat! You have every right to do a little jig of happiness.

However, we have the last and final mystery a turn of the page away now!

Summary

- Solving clues, we traveled to three exciting and historic places in the city:

  - **East End and Whitechapel:** The "poorer" boroughs of the east of the city may be historically associated with crime and poverty, but they have a unique artistic culture and vibe of their own.

  - **London Wall and Tower Hill:** Beware the Tower Hill tainted by associations of past executions. Despite its sinister past, it is a pretty place from where you can see the remains of the London Wall, built by the Romans and strengthened by the Anglo-Saxons, all around the city. It is a great place to study the gates that once led in and out of the city.

  - **The Tower of London and the Tower Bridge:** These two are culturally important as visible parts of London's architecture and crown. The Tower of London houses the crown jewels, but it was a royal residence, prison, fortress, and even a zoo at one point in time. The bridge, though constructed much later, matches the tower in architectural splendor and can offer you a spectacular view of the city.

And so we are almost there, super sleuth! We have come to the final case and adventure of this book! See you soon, victorious as always on the other side!

CHAPTER 5:

Uncovering the Secret Underground Drug Transport in London

Introduction

Detective, it's amazing that you have only one mystery to go now. You have pulled nothing short of a blinder (something achieved skillfully and faultlessly). But as always, let us have a butcher's hook (look) at the city and its story before morning on to the places and case.

The City: Gallivanting About

The English have a fun word, "gallivanting," which means "to move from one place to the next, enjoying yourself, and not worrying too much about responsibilities." Well, we have looked at the city's culture, history, diversity, and much more in the previous sections. However, the city's transportation facilities, world-class as they are, deserve a mention too. For what would London be without glimpses of the iconic black taxi cabs and the red double-decker buses, no?

London's wonderfully interconnected public transport enables people to move easily within the city without being too dependent on private transportation. Good public transport, including rail, road, water, and air transportation, is one of the hallmarks of a well-developed country, and London has it all. Apart from buses and taxis, London has an impressive array of ways to travel including the Underground, Tramlink, Light Railway, River Services, The Elizabeth Line, and the London Overground.

Interestingly, most of London's roads were made before cars. This is why they were too congested and had to be widened over the years. Cycling is also a well-loved way of getting from one place to another in the city. More than a million Londoners own their own bicycles, and bicycles are easily available for rent in the city.

London has an impressive fleet of buses, more than 8,700 to be specific, on which 6 million passengers travel every weekday. This is a huge improvement compared to the first omnibus service pulled by three horses on Marylebone Road in 1829, which could carry only 22 people (Transport for London, 2024 & Craig, 2017).

London's black taxis have an interesting story. They are driven by drivers who spend three years memorizing the city. They actually know every part of it like the back of their hands and without relying on maps or devices too! A strict test ensures that becoming a cab driver in London is no child's play. A rather recent addition to public road transport is the pedicab or the cycle rickshaw. However, these are limited to certain areas of the city.

London's Underground or Tube system has been operational since 1863. Over 1.35 billion passengers travel on the Tube every year, with 11 lines connecting 270 stations in central and suburban London. The "Underground" can be misleading because only 45% of the tracks are actually underground, while the rest of them run above the ground (TfL community Team, 2019).

The Docklands Light Railway is an automated, driverless railway system in east London that began in 1987. It has seven main branches and even connects to London City Airport. It has an impressive 45 stations and 149 vehicles (Transport for London, n.d.).

Tramlink is a tram and light railway system that serves the boroughs around the Croyden area. Starting in 1861, trams now cover 39 stops and carry 30 million passengers annually. Each tram can carry about 208 passengers at a time. Earlier horse-drawn, electric trams were introduced in 1901 (TfL Community Team, 2020).

Apart from Heathrow, the city's busiest airport, London has five other airports—Gatwick, Stansted, Luton, London City, and Southend. Many of these airports also provide Automated People Mover facilities or driverless vehicles that take passengers between the various parts of the airport.

Water services and canals which were once used to transport goods like coal and other resources are more used for leisure travel nowadays. Narrowboats and water buses are popular means of travel that people use.

And lastly, if you want some real fun, you can also try out the cloud cable cars in the city. You can move across the Thames from Greenwich to Royal Victoria Dock via the cable car. Apart from the novelty of using it, it also offers beautiful views of the city.

Now that you have an overview of London's wonderful transportation systems, let us dive straight into business.

The Mystery

Detective, this is the problem before you. A gang of smugglers has been transporting illegal drugs into the city! How have they been doing this right under the noses of the city authorities? Solve this puzzle to catch the criminals red-handed!

Chin Up!

We have a whole new case for you to solve. One last time, do take a long look at the rules of the game in the Introduction of Chapter 1.

Well, what are you waiting for? Ready, steady, go!

The Royal London Residence

Location: City of Westminster

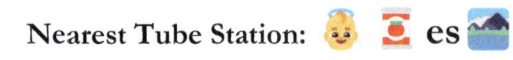

Nearest Tube Station: 👶 🇪 es 🏔️

Known as the monarch's official residence in London, Buckingham Palace has a history that goes way back. Initially, it wasn't even a palace. It was a house built for the Duke of Buckingham in 1703. King George III bought the residence for Queen Charlotte in 1762, after which it was called the "Queen's House". Only in the 1820s did a royal architect convert the house into a palace. The palace gardens were reshaped, and many of the courts were expanded. Queen Victoria was the first monarch to reside in the palace in 1837. Even after her time, subsequent monarchs made alterations to the building. The last such change was made during the time of King George V, the grandfather of Queen Elizabeth II. During WWII, the palace was bombed nine times, once when the King was in residence. The chapel of the palace was destroyed in the bombing. Footage of the king and queen inspecting the ruins was shown across theaters in the country to prove how the war affected the rich and poor alike. The chapel was never rebuilt, but in its place came the King's Gallery.

The palace has 775 rooms including 19 State Rooms. Every year, the monarch throws three garden parties at Buckingham Palace to which 30,000 people are invited (*Buckingham Palace,* n.d.).

Normally, Buckingham Palace is closed to visitors. An exception to this rule was in the mid-1990s when certain chambers were opened to the public for a fee used to finance the repairs of Windsor Castle, which was damaged by fire in 1992. You can tell if the king or queen is in residence at Buckingham Palace because the royal standard is flown above the palace during these times.

Since 1914, at least 12 people have entered Buckingham Palace without security clearance including a bloke (guy), Michael Fagan, who entered the queen's bedroom once. In 2007, unauthorized entry into the palace or its grounds was made a criminal offense.

When you get a chance to go near Buckingham Palace, don't forget to:

- Visit the King's Gallery, where objects of great value from the Royal Collection are displayed in the gallery, near the Royal Mews. It also boasts paintings and drawings by famous artists such as Leonardo da Vinci, Faberge, and others. A changing display of items from the Royal Collection ensures that visitors always have something new to see.

- Witness the iconic Changing of the Foot Guards or Changing of the Horse Guardd Ceremony at the palace, depending on the day of your visit.

- Take a peek at the room behind the famous balcony of the palace where Prince Charles and Princess Diana or Prince William and Princess Kate appeared after their weddings. The palace's East Wing has been opened to public tours for the first time in 2024!

Now, detective, you can tackle these trivia questions before moving on to the all-important mystery ones.

Fun and Trivia Questions

1. Why is Buckingham Palace ideally situated to be the main royal residence?

2. How large are the Buckingham Palace grounds? Is it closer to 40 acres or 100 acres?

3. How big is the ballroom of the palace? What was the first great event hosted by Buckingham Palace Ballroom? (Hint: The event was in 1856.)

4. Who protects the royal family while in residence?

5. Which is the oldest part of the palace? (It houses "spirits" not spooky.)

6. What do the Royal Mews hold? (Hint: The earlier occupants neighed, while the present ones "vroom".)

7. When the British say that everything is "hunky dory", what do they mean?

Well, let's hope you will solve the riddles below in a jiffy (quickly).

Riddles

One of the answers below is a clue to the next location.

- **Clue 1:** I am a rumored maze beneath the Buckingham Palace floors that might house secrets and people alike. What am I?

- **Clue 2:** Today, I may be the British Museum, but years ago I was not. In a famous Shakespearean romance with warring families, a name might strike you as very close to mine. Which building was I?

Let's hope you solved the clues without much of a kerfuffle (fuss) because we are now going to the next exciting place!

The First Public National Museum

Location: Great Russell Street, Bloomsbury

Nearest Tube Station: 🔴 🔥

The British Museum established in 1753 has been in existence for donkey's years (a very long time) and is older than the United States of America, which came into existence only in 1776! It is the world's oldest public museum and has the world's largest permanent collection of objects and items related to art, culture, and human history, numbering close to 8 million.

Initially, the museum started from the private collection of Sir Hans Sloane, an Anglo-Irish physician and naturalist. He expanded his collection of curiosities in his lifetime and left it to King George II after his time because he did not want the collection to be lost. At the time, he had a vast number of books, dried plants, prints, and drawings. He also had many historical artifacts from Africa, the Americas, Greece, Rome, the Middle East, and the Far East.

King George II established Sloane's collection as a public museum via an act of Parliament. The trustees in charge found and bought the Montagu House in Russell Street, Bloomsbury, as large enough to hold the collection for public viewership. Interestingly, they also considered Buckingham House for the same purpose, which they rejected in favor of the Montagu House. The Montagu House had to be expanded to house the collection. It was rebuilt in stages between 1823 and 1852. In 1759, the museum opened its reading room for scholars. The library was the largest part of the collection.

Over time, the collection got so large that it had to be shifted to two other buildings. What eventually became London's Natural History Museum was still officially called the British Museum (Natural History) until 1992. The British Library became a separate institution in 1973.

The British Museum has another "first" to its credit. It was one of the very first buildings to be almost completely electrified by 1889. The reason was that officials were worried that too many candles or lamps would burn down the ancient manuscripts and the building itself. Before electricity, the museum was forced to close down by early evening when it became too dark.

In the early 1900s, working at the museum was such a prestigious job that you had to take elaborate exams in history and other areas before you could be cleared to work there. The exams were a part of the Civil Service.

The museum has also been used as a setting for multiple films starting with *The Wakefield Cause* (1921). Another popular one in recent history has been *The Night at the Museum* (2014).

Being one of the earliest and largest colonizers, Britain had easy access to many of the valuables of other countries. There have also been many controversies surrounding objects the British Museum has refused to return to their countries of origin. The museum has the world's second-largest Egyptian mummy collection, after the Egyptian Museum in Cairo.

With a collection so vast and valuable, it is only natural that it would attract thieves and tricksters. In 2002, a Greek marble head sculpture went missing (Kennedy, 2002), while in 2004, somebody stole a rare jewelry collection from 700 AD containing earrings and other accessories (Kent, 2004)! A trickster only known as "Banksy" left a painting of a primitive man pushing a shopping trolley for all to see. It was several days before it was discovered and pulled down (Guidelines To Britain, 2019).

The British Museum is open every day, especially on weekends and holidays when it enjoys maximum visits. It has never charged visitors an entry fee. It stays open late on Fridays so that people can walk through and view the collection in a less rushed manner. It is the UK's most popular attraction, with 6.5 million people visiting annually (*29 things you (probably) didn't know...*, n.d.).

When in the museum, ensure you look at:

- The famous Egyptian Rosetta Stone and the mummies.

- The Lewis Chessmen, 12th-century chess pieces carved from walrus ivory.

- Aztec Serpent sculpture of a double-headed snake from 15th or 16th-century Mexico, made with turquoise set in wood.

Well, if you are not impressed by all that, I don't know what would excite you, detective. Now, it's time for the questions, and I hope you are prepared!

Fun and Trivia Questions

1. Who are some of the well-known painters whose works the British Museum contains?

2. What is special about the reading room of the museum?

3. Was there a museum tube station? What happened to it?

4. Which is a well-known Greek prized exhibit of the Museum? (Hint: It has something to do with marbles).

5. How many objects does the Museum display at one time?

6. What is something that once "came back to life" in the British Museum? How did this happen?

Now, the clue to our present case lies right ahead.

Riddles

Clue 3: Tell me, tell me, which of the museums we discuss in this chapter has a special Stamper Trail and why?

And now, it is time to move to the last two locations in London. One should interest you the most because it ties up with the introduction to the city we covered at the beginning of this chapter.

The Two Museums

You might well be wondering why we seem to be obsessed with so many museums at once in this last chapter of the adventure. The fact is that museums remind us of the history and culture of a city. The three museums we cover—the British Museum, Transport Museum, and Postal Museum—are only about ten minutes from each other by car. So, it does make sense to do the rounds at a single go, does it not?

London Transport Museum

Location: Covent Garden Piazza, opposite the main Covent Garden Market building

Nearest Tube Station: 👩‍🦳 🏠

As is obvious from its name, the Transport Museum is dedicated to all things related to the London Transport system, its history, and technological developments. Be prepared to be amazed by the types of vehicles that the city has seen over the ages.

Compared to the British Museum, the London Transport Museum is much newer. It has two main sites—the main one in Covent Garden and a depot in Acton. The Covent Garden Museum is open to the public every day, while the depot is a storage site of historic transportation artifacts and is only open on certain visitor days during the year.

Interestingly, the museum in Covent Garden is housed in what used to be an iron and glass building, which was part of the Covent Garden flower market. A large section of the museum consists of displays of old buses that have been retired from service. Similar displays of old railway cars and vehicles were introduced a little later. Today, you can see buses, rail carriages, trams, and trolleybuses from the 19th and 20th centuries. In fact, you can even see the first electric underground train from 1890!

When you visit make note of the:

- Hidden London tours, which are guided tours of railway stations that were abandoned in the 1990s. This tour gives you an opportunity to explore underground stations no longer used and otherwise closed to the public. You get a firsthand feel of stations like Aldwych, Down Street, and the secret sections of Piccadilly Circus, Charing Cross, and Euston stations. The tours also include rounds of Clapham South, which was used as a wartime shelter during German bombing. It is unique to experience London's history through its Underground.

- museum's virtual and simulated tours, which are an experience worth having.

- museum shop, especially if you are interested in collecting objects, posters, photos, or miniatures of vehicle models.

The Postal Museum

Location: Clerkenwell

Nearest Tube Station: 🔭 💍 don

Like the Transport Museum, which gives us a picture of London's history and culture through evolving transport facilities in the city, the Postal Museum does the same through the changing postal system of the country.

The Royal Mail is one of the oldest postal systems of the world, established in 1516 under King Henry VIII! It was only used for the delivery of royal posts until it was opened up for the public under King Charles I in 1635. Initially, the postage was always paid by the person receiving the letter. It was run by Thomas Witherings. Over the years, several people whom the Crown appointed ran the postal network in England. It was only in 1660, after the monarchy was re-established after the Civil War, that the postal network was established under state control.

In the 18th century, the postal network expanded, with mail coaches being used for sending and receiving letters between stations. It was in 1840 that the penny postage system was introduced, with the sender of the mail having to pay a single rate for the delivery of mail anywhere within the country. The adhesive stamp, called Penny Black, was introduced in the same year as visible proof of the fact that postage was paid by the sender.

In 1966, the National Postal Museum was opened in part because Reginald Phillips donated his philately collection of old stamps to the country. The museum opened to the public three years later in 1969. The museum receives an annual payment from the Royal Mail.

Today, you can see and be a part of:

- old postal uniforms, stamps, telegrams, vehicles used for the delivery of letters, and much more associated with the postal system of the country.

- events, workshops, and other educational programs.

And now, if your mind's not too boggled (amazed), let us get on with the trivia questions!

Fun and Trivia Questions

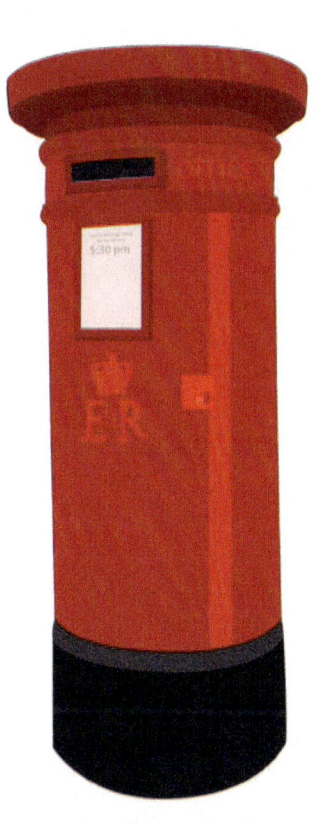

1. What is the fun fact about Angel Tube Station's escalator?

2. Which tube stations were named after pubs near them?

3. Why was the Tube more popular and developed in North London than it was in the South?

4. A credit card-sized card acts as a ticket for people to travel on the London Underground, London Overground, Docklands Light Railway, Tramlink, London Buses, and National Rail services in the Greater London area. What is this magic card called?

5. When and where was the first post office pillar box erected?

6. Postboxes were preceded by a person who collected letters. What was he called?

7. Apart from red, what other colors were postboxes painted?

And now, travel detective we have come to the final clue of the book!

Riddles

Solve this final clue to find how the criminals have been secretly transporting drugs into the city.

Clue 4, Answer to the Mystery: The newer of the two last museums holds an age-old secret of secret carriages that can run driverless! Psst! My name is made of two rhyming words.

Solve this clue to find out how to stop the smugglers!

The Big Reveal

Jolly good work, detective! You really deserve credit for solving all these puzzles with grit and guts!

Take some time out to break a leg (celebrate) now!

Summary

- In this last chapter, we visited four locations, with three of them being museums!
    - **Buckingham Palace:** This is one of the most culturally significant landmarks of the city because the king and queen stay here when they are in London. Though not open to the public, the gallery of the palace is open.
    - **The British Museum:** The world's oldest public museum, it contains a huge collection of various types of books, objects, and other things. Take your time around this treasure trove of artifacts.
    - **The London Transport Museum:** This museum is a great place to learn the history of transport in the country.
    - **The Postal Museum in London:** As a tribute to the postal system of the country, it is a great way to understand the changes that happened in communication systems.

Adios, detective. Hopefully, we can catch up soon in another city in this big wide world!

CONCLUSION

Detective, you've done it! You've journeyed through the bustling streets, hidden alleyways, and iconic landmarks of London, unraveling mysteries that have challenged even the most seasoned sleuths. From the whispers of the Cabinet Office to the Postal Museum, you've shown that you're not just a visitor but a true detective with a sharp mind and an adventurous spirit.

Throughout the *Travel Guide for Kids: Mystery Adventure Tour of London*, you've been on a unique journey. Each chapter presented a new problem, a fresh mystery intertwined with the rich history and culture of one of the world's most fascinating cities. You've learned that London is more than just a collection of famous sites—it's a city alive with stories, both well-known and hidden, waiting to be told.

But, as any great detective knows, the end of one mystery often marks the beginning of another. London never stands still, with new stories and secrets emerging every day. Perhaps you've noticed something that wasn't fully explained—a detail that caught your eye or a riddle that seemed to lead to another question. That's the beauty of London; it always leaves you wanting more, always beckoning you to dig deeper.

And while you've brought to light many of London's secrets, there's always more to explore. Perhaps one day you'll return to these streets, or maybe your next adventure will take you to another city, one with its own mysteries and stories waiting to be discovered. Wherever you go, take with you the skills you've honed and the curiosity that has driven you through this journey.

Share your discoveries with friends and family. Tell them about the hidden corners of London, the riddles you solved, and the excitement of piecing together the clues. Who knows? Your stories might inspire them to embark on their own adventure, turning them into detectives eager to discover the world's hidden wonders.

As you close this book, remember that the adventure doesn't have to end. Keep your eyes open, your mind sharp, and your detective kit close at hand. London may have revealed many of its secrets to you, but the world is full of mysteries just waiting to be solved by a detective like you.

Until we meet again on the next great mystery hunt—happy investigating!

TRIVIA AND FUN ANSWERS

Chapter 1: Trivia and Fun Answers

The Ministerial Offices

Nearest Tube Station: Westminster

1. 300 years. 10 Downing Street has been the official residence of British Prime Ministers since 1735, when Robert Walpole became the first Lord of the Treasury. The house was gifted to him by King George II. However, Walpole refused to accept it as a personal gift and instead asked the king to make it an official residence for Lords of the Treasury. By 2025, British prime ministers will have lived and worked from here for close to 290 years.

2. In 1908. when Herbert Asquith was the Prime Minister, the door of 10 Downing Street was painted dark green, not black. It isn't clear why this paint was chosen. There are rumors such as his wife, Lady Asquith, did not like black color, or perhaps it was a matter of style. Back then, bronze green was a popular color choice for doors.

3. When World War II broke out, Neville Chamberlain was the Prime Minister. He continued to serve till 1940. However, Winston Churchill stepped in in 1940, and he is considered to be the Prime Minister who led the nation to victory against the Germans.

4. Mr. Chicken was the last nonpolitical resident of 10 Downing Street. History doesn't tell us much about him, but he moved out of the house just before Robert Walpole moved into it.

5. Usually, 15-25 people serve in the UK Cabinet in various positions. The 2024 Cabinet led by Sir Keir Starmer as PM has 22 members.

6. Many of England's former colonies like India continue to use the same or a similar structure of government with two houses. Other examples include Canada, Australia, New Zealand, and several more.

7. A kitchen cabinet includes the unofficial advisors of the government. You may think that most decisions are made within the walls of the Cabinet Office Rooms. However, many prime ministers have advisors, not in the cabinet, who help them make important decisions. Many of these decisions are already made before they come to the cabinet rooms.

8. Charing Cross station is also near the Cabinet Office.

9. The UK flag is called the Union Jack or Union Flag because it represents the crosses of England, Wales, Scotland, and Northern Ireland.

The London Eye

Nearest Tube station: Waterloo

1. The London Eye has 32 capsules, one for each borough in London. They are numbered from 1-33. Number 13 is left out because it has always been associated with bad luck. Each capsule can hold 25 people, and each person can carry a selfie stick too.

2. A spin on the London Eye takes about 30 minutes to complete. On a clear day, you can see all the way to Windsor Castle.

3. The London Eye is the largest cantilevered observation wheel, which means that it is supported only on one side. The Orlando Eye in Orlando, Florida, in the US is also another cantilevered wheel.

4. The London Eye spins at a speed of 0.9 km (0.6 mi) per hour, which is twice as fast as a tortoise sprinting.

5. In 2013, marking Queen Elizabeth II's 60th year as queen, one of the capsules was renamed the Coronation Capsule. This is the only capsule that looks different and is painted red.

6. The London Eye weighs 1000 tonnes (t) or 1 million pounds (lb). An average person weighs between 130–180 lb.

7. The London Eye is lit up in different colors for different celebrations. For instance, on St. Patrick's Day, it is lit up in green, while for Princess Kate and Prince William's wedding in 2011, it was blue and white.

Big Ben and the Houses of Parliament

Nearest Tube Station: Westminster

1. The Big Ben is the largest four-faced clock in the world. Big Ben's clock dials and hands are Prussian blue and gold, and the surrounding areas feature the colors of the British flag: red, white, and blue.

2. If you wish to climb all the way from the ground to the belfry of the tower, you would need to take 334 steps!

3. The tower housing the clock and the bell was simply called the Clock Tower originally. Now, it has been renamed the Elizabeth Tower after the Diamond Jubilee celebrations of Queen Elizabeth II in 2012.

4. Westminster Quarters is the tune that the four smaller bells of the clock tower play to mark every 15 minutes of an hour. It is also known as the Westminster Chimes, Cambridge Quarters, or Cambridge Chimes because it was originally composed at the Church of St Mary the Great, Cambridge.

5. The doorkeepers of the House of Commons always keep a snuff box with them because smoking has been banned within the chamber since the late 17th century. Snuff is the only permitted form of tobacco that can be used. It is the duty of the Principal Doorkeeper of the Palace of Westminster to keep the snuff box stocked and ready.

6. The Gunpowder Treason Plot of 1605 was a failed attempt to murder King James I by blowing up the House of Lords. It was led by Guy Fawkes and others, who were captured and killed by hanging. November 5th is Guy Fawkes Day in England. Figures of Guy Fawkes, bonfires, and crackers are lit up all over the country. The story of Guy Fawkes has also inspired movies like *V For Vendetta* (2005).

7. A vote in each house is called a division because the MPs have to get up and walk to the right corridor in their house. They say "aye" and "no" in the House of Commons and "in favor" and "not In favor" in the House of Lords.

Chapter 2: Trivia and Fun Answers

The Square Mile

1. Hyde Park has a pet cemetery dating from 1880, having about 300 lots.

2. Trafalgar Square has so many pigeons that there has been a rule against feeding them since 2003. They are sometimes called "flying rats" because of their nuisance.

3. The black cabs of London are a signature part of London roads. There is no conclusive evidence to explain why they were called "hackney" carriages when horse-drawn carriages were the main mode of public transport. A French word "haquenée" might be a clue because it meant a horse of medium height suitable for carrying ladies. There is a borough of Hackey, but since the area was marshy and unsuitable for keeping horses, many wonder if the two terms are related at all.

4. Mary Poppins is the magical English nanny in the book series by P.L. Travers. Though the original 1934 book was popular, people now remember Disney's 1964 film version of it more. It featured Julie Andrews as Mary Poppins.

5. London Heathrow is the busiest airport in the UK. In 1930, it began as a small airfield and was later expanded after World War II. Heathrow's Terminal 5 has a large "ghost station" beneath it. It was built alongside the terminal in 2008 to link the airport to the rail network. However, the work was not completed, and even the rails were not laid.

6. The London Underground or the Tube was opened in 1863 as the world's first underground passenger railway network or subway. Initially, before electrification, gas-lit carriages and steam engines were used, and passengers would collapse because of the heat and smoke. By 1890, the Underground was electrified.

7. Numbers 23 and 24 Leinster Gardens look like regular houses on the street but are only 5 ft thick. These house fronts were built to hide the old railway lines from public view.

The Studio of Magic

Nearest Railway Station: Watford Junction

1. When J. K. Rowling was on vacation in the village of Lacock, she met an old man with a dog named Harry. She was also staying next to a pottery shop. Putting these two together, she came up with "Harry Potter."

2. The Duke and Duchess of Cambridge, William and Kate, and Prince Harry attended the grand opening of the London Warner Bros Studio Tours in April 2013. Several of the movie's cast and crew also appeared at the event. J. K. Rowling was also present.

3. About 6000 people can visit the Studio Tours daily. However, the guided tours are for smaller groups of around eight people.

4. The House Points Counter in the Great Hall are huge glass tubes, which fill with beads colored in the house colors (Green for Slytherin, Red for Gryffindor, Yellow for Hufflepuff, and Blue for Ravenclaw) depending on the points earned by the house. The building of these led to a shortage of Indian glass beads over the country.

5. The Ministry of Magic is one of the largest sets created for the movies and can fit 50 London buses inside its atrium. It took 22 weeks to complete construction.

6. J. K. Rowling created many unique words in her books. The non-magical people, such as Hermoine Granger's parents, are referred to as "muggles" in the books and movies.

The Stone of Brutus: The Heart of London

Nearest Tube Station: Cannon Street

1. Today, the London Stone is only 53 cm tall, 43 cm wide, and 30 cm thick. However, a Frenchman, L Grenade, visiting the city in 1578 described it as being 3 ft high, 2 ft wide, and 1 ft thick (91 cm X 60 cm X 30 cm).

2. Cannon Street was originally Candlewick Street because the street was known for the candlemakers on it. With the Cockney dialect that many of the lower classes used, Candlewick Street probably got shortened over time to Canwick Street, Cannik Street, and Cannon Street.

3. The London Stone was moved from the middle of the road to the curbside because it was causing problems for the traffic. Carts that crashed into the stone either lost their wheels or the wheels shattered to bits.

4. Dr John Dee, who was an astrologer, occultist, and adviser to Queen Elizabeth I, was so fascinated by the magical powers the London Stone was supposed to have that he lived near it for a while and is said to have broken off pieces of it for alchemical experiments. Alchemy was the medieval branch of science that was obsessed with trying to convert other materials into gold.

5. King Arthur is a mythical king of England who is said to have battled with dragons and led a band of heroes called the Knights of the Round Table, and he has been credited with uniting the people of England under one country. Arthur's magical sword, Excalibur, helped him in all of his adventures. It

is said that Arthur first drew the Excalibur from inside the London Stone where it was stuck. No other person could draw it but him, making him the unquestioned king.

6. The plaque confirms that the purpose of the stone is unknown, though it does guess that perhaps it was part of the Roman buildings.

Chapter 3: Trivia and Fun Answers

Scotland Yard

Nearest Tube Station: Westminster

1. Arthur Conan Doyle's Sherlock Holmes frequently worked with Detective Inspector Lestrade of Scotland Yard, while Agatha Christie's Hercule Poirot often helped Inspector Japp. Of course, the Scotland Yard officers in these books (and their screen adaptations) were never quite as brilliant as the private detectives, who always beat them to solve the crime.

2. The Scotland Yard has a secret museum called the Crime Museum, nicknamed the Black Museum. This contains evidence collected from crime scenes. Some of the objects in the collection are said to be too disturbing for the public to see, so the museum remains closed to the public. A celebrity might bag a special invite. Arthur Conan Doyle, author of *Sherlock Holmes*, has supposedly visited the museum.

3. The English did not use the forensic method of collecting and matching prints until 1901, when Sir Edward Henry, the assistant commissioner of Scotland Yard, established the Metropolitan Police Fingerprint Bureau. A year later, a thief who stole billiard balls was caught by the fingerprint he left on a windowsill. In 1904, Scotland Yard showed the effectiveness of fingerprinting at the St. Louis World's Fair, helping American law enforcement agents learn this new science.

4. Patrol officers in London never carried a gun till 1994! With increased assaults on unarmed police officers, a few select officers, especially those called in response to high-risk calls, were permitted to carry guns from 1994 onwards. Ninety percent of the Met officers still go unarmed (which means only 10% are armed), because very few Britishers own a firearm!

5. Scotland Yard employs a team of "super recognizers," talented in associating faces with names, relying only on their memory. These officers are selected through a facial recognition test introduced by Harvard in 2009. For instance, Constable Gary Collins recognized 180 out of 4,000 individuals while looking at video footage from the 2011 London riots, while facial recognition software could identify only one.

Britain's Valhalla

Nearest Tube Station: St. James Park

1. There's nothing peculiar about the Westminster Abbey. A Royal Peculiar means property that belongs to the monarchy or the throne. The Westminster Abbey is a Royal Peculiar and belongs to the King or Queen of England and not to the Church of England. It is supported by money from tourists rather than donations to the church.

2. More than 3,300 people are buried at the church. Earlier, it was only open to royalty or the famous. But slowly, it was opened to anybody who could afford to be buried there.

3. Westminster Abbey has Britain's oldest door, or the only remaining Anglo-Saxon door in the country. The door dates back to the year 1050. A scientific dating technique showed the door was built from a tree in Hainault, which grew there between 924 and 1030. Another surprising thing found was that the covering on the door was possibly human skin.

4. Westminster Abbey boasts of the highest ceiling in the UK, measuring 102 ft from the ground! The regular London double-decker bus is 39 ft and 4 in.

5. The beautiful pavement before the High Altar of Westminster Abbey was constructed in 1268 under King Henry III. Artisans from Rome made this extraordinary surface using materials like onyx, colored glass, mosaic, and marble. On it, one can find three slightly readable inscriptions that refer to the apocalypse, or the end of the world in 19,683 years.

6. In 1296, the Stone of Destiny, also called the Stone of Scone, was transported to Westminster Abbey from Scotland by King Edward I. He wanted the stone to be placed beneath the Coronation Chair. On Christmas Eve in 1950, four students from Glasgow broke into the church and took the stone. Luckily, the stone was recovered and found buried in a field in Kent. It was returned to Scotland in 1996, after 700 years!

The Garden of the Abbey and Convent

1. Inigo Jones designed the Covent Garden based on the grand piazzas of Europe. It had portico houses to the north and east with continuous arcades running beneath them. You can think of it like a continuous passageway. These houses were quickly bought by the aristocracy who wanted nothing better than the latest European-style houses.

2. Both the Theater Royal and the Royal Opera House are said to be haunted. While the theater has often witnessed the "Man in Grey," an 18th-century nobleman believed to have been stabbed to death in the theater, the Opera House is supposed to have its in-house poltergeist who threw debris at workers when restoration work was happening in 1999.

3. The oldest pub is the Lamb and Flag established in the early 18th century. It is nicknamed "Bucket of Blood" because of the violent and bloody fights that used to happen between the customers.

4. The *Punch and Judy* show, a very famous street show that was put up for kids, was first recorded in the diary of Samuel Pepys in 1662.

5. The pineapple was used to represent Covent Garden. Not being native to England, pineapples were considered to be an exotic fruit at one time.

6. John Montagu, known also as the Earl of Sandwich, was the first to request a meal that wouldn't require him to get up from his seat or dirty his hand, while continuing to gamble. The kitchen staff brought him a slice of meat placed between two slices of bread. This was in 1762 at a social club called the Beef Steak Club, located on the now-lost Wych Street, off Drury Lane in Covent Garden. Unknowingly, they created a most beloved lunchtime dish—the sandwich.

7. "Apples and pears" is a reference to steps or a staircase in Cockney slang. The idea is that fruit sellers often arrange their fruits (apples and pears) on steps.

Chapter 4: Trivia and Fun Answers

East End and White Chapel

1. Fagin is the old miser who lived off other people. He was a miser who lent space for sleeping to homeless boys in exchange for them picking pockets and other criminal activities. People who use children for illegal activities are still called "Fagin".

2. Altab Ali Park, Alder Street is the park where the church was located. St Mary Matfelon was destroyed in World War II. The park, which was originally called St. Mary's Park, was renamed in 1988 in honor of Altab Ali, a young Bangladeshi who was stabbed to death in a racist attack in the city.

3. Harrods was established by Charles Henry Harrod as a wholesale grocery store in Stepney in the East End. Starting in a small room with two assistants and a messenger boy, the business soon grew into a successful retail store selling perfumes, medicines, fruits, vegetables, and stationery. Harrods also owns real estate, aviation, and investment companies. Harrods is presently owned by the state of Qatar today.

4. The gate was removed in 1761 to improve traffic flow. Aldgate's name probably comes from the "old gate," "East Gate", or even "Ale Gate," as there was possibly an ale house nearby. It was a huge gate in the London Wall that was built by the Romans. It was rebuilt several times in the 12th, 13th, and 17th centuries.

5. Archaeologists found a 1,900-year-old Roman sculpture in Minories, Aldgate, in 2013. It was found in what was Roman London's "Eastern Cemetery." The statue was 65 cm tall and was that of an eagle with a snake in its beak. It was named "The Minories Eagle", and it is one of the rarest and finest artifacts.

6. The "Elephant Man" was Joseph Merrick, who lived from 1862–1890. He became well known in Whitechapel for his bodily deformities making his skin look like that of an elephant. He was exhibited in a shop on Whitechapel Road before being helped by Frederick Treves from the Royal London Hospital opposite the shop. There is a museum in the hospital about Merrick's life.

7. "Ruby Murray" is Cockney slang for "curry." They are asking you whether you would like to have curry for dinner.

The Wall and Tower Hill

Nearest Tube Station: Tower Hill

1. The churches around the area were named to give you an idea whether they were within or outside the wall. If a church name contains "within" (e.g., St Martin within Ludgate), it means it was inside the wall, and if the name contains "without" (St Sepulchre without Newgate), you would know that you're outside of the wall.

2. Just opposite the Museum of London is Noble Street where you can see the remains of the London Wall. This section was uncovered after the German bombing of London in the 1940s. You can see parts of the wall as well as one of the sentry towers in the south side.

3. Near St Giles Cripplegate Tower is the remains of the Barber-Surgeons' Hall Tower. The tower was built in the 13th century. Later in 1607, the Barber-Surgeons' company built a new hall into the edge of the wall, incorporating the old tower as an apse.

4. All Hallows Church, built in 1767 near Bishopsgate, has a vestry built into the foundation of the London Wall's bastion. In front of the church you can see some sections of the wall.

5. Bishopsgate was known for displaying the heads of newly executed prisoners on its spikes. It was an original Roman gate rebuilt during the Middle Ages.

6. The Roman wall at Duke's Place is located inside a subway. The subway walls still contain both the Roman as well as the later Medieval walls. They were discovered during excavations in 1977.

7. Geoffrey Chaucer, the Father of English poetry, lived in rooms above Aldgate when he was working as a customs official. No part of this gate survives because it was pulled down in 1760 to allow better movement of traffic.

The Bridge and the Royal Fortress

Nearest Tube Station: Tower Hill

1. Tower Bridge is often confused with London Bridge, which is 10 minutes away. A legend claims a Viking leader destroyed the London Bridge in 1014 by attaching cables to its wooden pilings and then sailing away. Though there's no record of this attack, the song could be a reference to this. History has seen the London Bridge in poor condition several times, and the song could be a more general reference to this fact as well.

2. The Yeoman Warders of the Tower of London have a special ceremony to lock up the Tower every evening. Come rain or shine, the Ceremony of the Keys, as it is called, has happened for 700 years.

3. The crown jewels include St Edward's Crown, the crown used for coronation.

4. Long ago, the wages of the warders were said to be paid in part as a ration of beef. This is probably where the term "Beefeater" originates. All Yeoman Warders are retired members of the armed services even today.

5. The Tower Bridge is red, white, and blue, painted in honor of Queen Elizabeth II's Silver Jubilee in 1977. Inside, the Tower Bridge retains its original chocolate brown, which was Queen Victoria's favorite color.

6. Prince of Wales is the Heir Apparent to the throne. Prince William is Prince of Wales after the connotation of King Charles III.

Chapter 5: Trivia and Fun Answers

The Royal London Residence

Nearest Tube Station: St. James Park

1. Buckingham Palace sits in the very heart of London, surrounded by the lavish St. James's and Green Parks. It is the perfect place for the king or queen.

2. The palace grounds are 39 acres or 16 hectares in all.

3. 36.6 m long, 18 m wide, and 13.5 m high (120 ft X 59 ft X 45 ft), the ballroom is the largest room in the palace. The first event ever to be held in the magnificent ballroom was a celebration of the end of the Crimean War in 1856.

4. King Henry VII made the Royal Body Guard or the King's Guard infantry that protects Buckingham Palace and St. James's Palace. They have done their duty for 500 years now. The Changing of the Guard ceremony happens at the Buckingham Palace Forecourt every Monday, Wednesday, Friday, and Sunday.

5. The wine vaults (spirits also refer to alcohol), located beneath the West Wing, are the oldest part of the palace. These vaults belonged to the Duke of Buckingham way before the residence became a royal residence.

6. Next to the palace is the Royal Mews, where the royal carriages, including the Gold State Coach, are held. This rococo gilt coach, designed in 1760, was first used for the State Opening of Parliament by George III in 1762 and has been used for every coronation since that of William IV. It was also used for the coronation of King Charles III and Queen Camilla recently. In the mews, you will also find the cars used by the royal family and the coach horses used at royal ceremonial processions.

7. "Hunky-dory" generally means that everything is going according to plan and that there are no hitches or problems.

The First Public National Museum

Nearest Tube Station: Holburn

1. The museum has the works of Michelangelo, Da Vinci, Munch, Van Gogh, Hogarth, Rembrandt, Picasso, and so many more artists.

2. Located at the center of the Great Court, the circular reading room has a diameter of over 42 m. In total, it contains over 4.5 km of bookcases and 40 km of shelves. Though it originally contained a large collection of books, after the books were moved to the British Library, the Reading Room is now used for special exhibitions.

3. Yes. For 33 years, the British Museum had its own underground tube station, making the Museum more accessible to those living in nearby regions. The Museum Station was closed by the end of 1933 because the newly built Holborn Station was only 100 yards away.

4. The Parthenon Sculptures or the Elgin Marbles were removed in 1801 from the Parthenon, a temple dedicated to Goddess Athena, in Athens, Greece. They were shipped to England by arrangements made by Thomas Bruce, 7th Lord Elgin.

5. The museum displays roughly 80,000 objects at any one time. This is only 1% of the collection. The displays include many of the most important items. Many objects within the collection cannot be on permanent display because they are light-sensitive.

6. The most famous case of suspended animation was that of a snail, which was part of a collection of snails donated to the natural history collection of the museum in 1846. The snail was on display for four years before people noticed it was alive. It was moved to a more suitable living condition but died six years later.

The Museums

Nearest Tube Station to London Transport Museum: Covent Garden

Nearest Tube Station to Postal Museum London: Farringdon

1. The Angel Tube Station has Western Europe's longest escalator, with 318 steps.

2. Elephant & Castle, Angel, Swiss Cottage, Royal Oak, and Manor House Stations were all named after pubs.

3. The Underground serves North London more than South London due to factors like unfavorable land, historical competition from surface railways, and the historical development of London, which was always more focused to the north of the River Thames. South London is served mainly by surface railways.

4. The Oyster Card is an electronic card and ticket which can be used to pay for many forms of transportation in the Greater London Area.

5. The first Post Office pillar box, where people could deposit their letters, was erected in 1852 in Jersey. Pillar boxes in mainland Britain were introduced in 1853.

6. Before the postbox existed, people would either take their letters to a Receiving House or wait for the bellman. The bellman, dressed in a special uniform, rang a bell to let people know he would collect their mail.

7. When postboxes were introduced in 1852, they were painted red. However, later postboxes were green. This was an issue as people had trouble finding them, camouflaged against greenery. They were changed back to red in 1874.

ANSWERS TO THE MYSTERY

Each of the answers below will slowly reveal the mystery piece by piece until the puzzle is solved with the final clue.

Chapter 1

Ans Clue 1: The unicorn is the one-horned, magical creature on the UK coat of arms. This imaginary animal was considered strong, brave, and untamable. It was originally a part of the royal Scottish coat of arms and Scottish national animal. This clue is a red herring, not contributing to the mystery.

Ans Clue 2: Rats carried a bacteria that resulted in the spread of the Bubonic Plague, which killed 100,000 people in 1665–1666. Keep in mind, the intruder is somehow related to the rat.

Ans Clue 3: Wenlock and Mandeville were the official mascots for the 2012 Summer Olympics and the Summer Paralympics, respectively. London hosted both of these events. The mascots are both one-eyed (like the lens of a camera) and have small, yellow lights on their head, symbolic of the London taxis. This clue is a red herring and does not contribute to the final mystery.

Ans Clue 4: Cats are said to have nine lives. This is partly because of their mystical nature and ability to survive, and they are worshipped in certain cultures. A cat is the greatest foe of the mouse.

Ans Clue 5: Larry the Cat, Chief Mouser at 10 Downing Street, keeps mice away. The cat was already an answer to clue 4. Larry has been a member of 10 Downing Street staff since 2011 and is the first cat to be given that title officially. He was a stray cat adopted from the Battersea Dogs & Cats Home, mainly to become a pet for PM David Cameron's children.

Answer to Clue 6 and the Mystery: *We are mice intruders at the Cabinet Offices, chased by Larry. The mouse is biologically a cousin of the rat, answer to Riddle 2.*

Chapter 2

Ans Clue 1: Cannons were used to fire at enemies. Cannon Street is the only clue linked to the London stone.

Ans Clue 2: "Diagonally." Diagon Alley is the street from where all the Hogwarts supplies were bought. This clue leads to the next location but does not contribute further to the mystery.

Ans Clue 3: 221B Baker Street was the fictionalized residence of Sherlock Holmes, where today you will find a memorial house in tribute to him. This clue is a red herring thrown in only to confuse.

Ans Clue 4: This London Stone on the Isle of Grain, beside Yantlet Creek, is one of many boundary stones that stand beside the rivers Thames and Medway. These were used to mark the jurisdiction limits and the fishing rights of London City. There are such London stones in Staines, Upnor, and Crowstone too. This London Stone is a red herring.

Ans Clue 5: This is London Stone on Cannon Street, which holds all the mystery related to the safety and security of London.

Answer to Clue 6 and the Mystery: *The Palladium was an ancient wooden statue of Pallas, the Roman city of Troy's patron deity. It offered Troy protection from invaders and other types of dangers. Moving or destroying the Palladium from its position right outside the entrance to the city was believed to bring destruction or bad luck to Troy. Similarly, legends say that the London Stone is the heart of the city—destroying or moving it from its location is believed to bring ill omen upon London.*

Chapter 3

Ans Clue 1: College Garden is a private garden of Westminster Abbey, London, open to the public between 10.00 a.m. and 4.00 p.m., Monday to Friday.

Ans Clue 2: St. Dunstan in the East Church is now a public garden built over the ruins of the church, which was destroyed in the Blitz. This is a red herring and does not contribute to the mystery.

Ans Clue 3: The London Coliseum, or the Coliseum Theatre, is a theatre in St. Martin's Lane, Westminster, built as one of London's largest and most luxurious "family" theatres that opened in 1904. The Colosseum in Rome, Italy, is the largest ancient amphitheater ever built. Despite its age, it is still the largest standing amphitheater in the world. The Coliseum is very close to the mystery location.

Ans Clue 4: The Theater Royal on Drury Lane, Covent Garden, is the oldest theater site to be in continuous use. It was established in 1663, more than 350 years ago. However, its building was rebuilt several times because of fires and for the sake of renovations. The present building was built in 1812.

Answer to Clue 5 and the Mystery: *Brydges Place is especially narrow, being just 1 ft 3 in. (0.38 m) wide at its narrowest point. It is commonly claimed to be the narrowest street in London. It runs along the Coliseum you have already named in Clue 3. This is where the tourists are.*

Chapter 4

Clue 1: Bethlehem Hospital, first established in Bishopsgate in 1247, was the first mental asylum in England. It was called "Bedlam" and was infamous for the brutal treatment of its patients, so it soon developed a fearsome reputation. Interestingly, during its construction, the London Wall to the East was made a part of the walls of Bedlam. Or rather, it was built into a part of the London Wall. Presently, Bethlehem Hospital is located in Bromley and is one of the leading institutions in the research and cure of mental ailments.

Clue 2: Previously, Tower Hill was used as a site for public executions. After this was stopped, Trinity Square and Gardens were laid out in 1797 by Samuel Wyatt, a famous English architect and engineer. He used the square and gardens as the backdrop for Trinity House, completed a year earlier.

Clue 3: The Tower of London, which holds the Crown Jewels, has been all of these places mentioned. This place is linked to the mystery to be solved.

Clue 4: The London Bridge is different from the Tower Bridge, though often confused with it. Both the bridges are within walking distance of each other and only about 1 km apart. This is a red herring and does not contribute to the mystery.

Answer to Clue 5 and the Mystery: *The six famous ravens at their lodgings on the South Lawn at the Tower of London are known as the guardians of the Tower. According to traditional belief, their presence protects the Crown and the Tower. A wide-held superstition is that if the Tower of London ravens are lost or fly away, the monarchy and Britain will fall. The names of the current Tower Ravens are Jubilee, Harris, Poppy, Georgie, Edgar, Branwen, and Rex.*

Chapter 5

Clue 1: A series of secret tunnels are said to run beneath Buckingham Palace, connecting it to Whitehall, King James's Castle, and other locations. There is a story that when the Queen Mother and King George VI descended into the tunnels, they met a man from Newcastle who was living in the tunnels. This clue is a red herring though, and its truth has never been established.

Clue 2: The Montagu House became the British Museum. Shakespeare's *Romeo and Juliet* features the warring families of the hero and heroine—the Montagues and the Capulets.

Clue 3: The London Transport Museum is laid out around a route with the Stamper Trail, a series of 13 stamping stations where people can stamp the card they are given at the entrance. This is to give people a feel of olden times when tickets were actually stamped on public transport to show that they were used once.

Answer to Clue 4 and the Mystery: *The Postal Museum established in 2004 is newer than the Transport Museum established in 1980. The "Mail Rail" were electric carriages of the Royal Mail that carried letters and mail from one sorting house to the other from 1927 to 2003, when it was shut down. These driverless carriages traveled in narrow tunnels that were only 70 feet wide. It was shut down because, by 2003, mails were replaced by communication systems like emails and SMS. The Mail Rail was partly reopened in 2017 as part of the Postal Museum Tour for the public, and you can take a ride on it!*

ABOUT THE AUTHOR

Elizabeth Anne resides and works in Switzerland. She is British and has lived in and visits London regularly. She has a deep connection with children that has been part of her nature from a very young age. Her experience teaching children from diverse cultural backgrounds such as Japanese, Chinese, Malay and Filipino, has reinforced her belief that play is not merely a break from learning but the very essence of serious childhood education. She wholeheartedly echoes Diane Ackerman's profound words, asserting that play is, indeed, the brain's preferred mode of assimilating knowledge.

While Elizabeth Anne trained in the Montessori teaching approach, her professional journey led her into the realm of people management, specifically Human Resources Management. She has traveled widely to different countries in Europe, South America, Africa, and Asia, and lived in Cameroon, Pakistan, Malaysia, Uganda, and Columbia. This has given her a broad perspective and panoramic view of various cultures and societies.

An avid bibliophile herself, she cherishes fond memories of engrossing her son as he was growing up, in late-night reading escapades, only to find him eagerly awaiting the continuation of the literary journey at the crack of dawn the following morning.

Recognizing the sanctity of quality family bonding, Elizabeth Anne enjoys curating memorable family vacations. Her writing resonates with a zest for nurturing young minds, fostering family ties, and enjoying the journey of growth and exploration that life has to offer.

References

About London Transport Museum. (n.d.). London Transport Museum. https://www.ltmuseum.co.uk/about

Allen, L. (2017, November 3). *The London Stone*. Jane Austen's London. https://janeaustenslondon.com/2017/11/03/the-london-stone/

A ride for your imagination | An unmissable day out for everyone only at The Postal Museum. (n.d.). The Postal Museum. https://www.postalmuseum.org/

Barnaby, J. (2020, April 21). *20 interesting facts about London's Tower Bridge*. London X London. https://www.londonxlondon.com/tower-bridge-facts/

Barrow, M. (2024). *London, England - Facts about London for kids*. Project Britain. https://projectbritain.com/london/b.html#google_vignette

Barzey, U. P. (2015, July 17). *11 facts about Westminster Abbey*. Guide London. https://www.guidelondon.org.uk/blog/major-london-sites/11-facts-about-westminster-abbey/

Bibby, M. (2024, April 5). *London Stone: the "Heart of London."* Historic UK. https://www.historic-uk.com/HistoryUK/HistoryofEngland/London-Stone/

BBC. (2016, December 19). *Gardeners' question time - 10 surprising facts about number 10 Downing Street*. BBC. https://www.bbc.co.uk/programmes/articles/3LrMh99XJ1Xsh7GtrvH1s8H/10-surprising-facts-about-number-10-downing-street

Beckman, B. (2022, August 26). *Eye on London - Visiting the London Eye with kids*. Little Kid Big City. https://littlekidbigcity.com/eye-on-london-riding-the-london-eye-with-kids/

Buckingham Palace. (n.d.). Britannica Kids. https://kids.britannica.com/kids/article/Buckingham-Palace/476233

CityDays. (2023, June 21). *London Wall, London, England*. Citydays.com. https://citydays.com/places/london-wall/

Clout, H. D., Hebbert, M. J., & Ehrlich, B. (2024, August 13). *London*. Encyclopedia Britannica. https://www.britannica.com/place/London

Covent Garden facts for kids. (2019). Kiddle. https://kids.kiddle.co/Covent_Garden#Landmarks

Craig, Z. (2017, January 10). *16 things you might not know about London's buses*. Londonist. https://londonist.com/2016/09/london-bus-facts

East End of London facts for kids. (n.d.). Kiddle. https://kids.kiddle.co/East_End_of_London

London Mother Editorial Team. (2019, November 4). *24 fascinating London facts for kids*. The London Mother. https://www.thelondonmother.net/london-facts-for-kids/

Editors of Encyclopaedia (2024 a, June 27). Tower Bridge. *Encyclopedia Britannica*. https://www.britannica.com/topic/Tower-Bridge

Editors of Encyclopaedia (2024, August 9). *Scotland Yard*. Encyclopedia Britannica. https://www.britannica.com/topic/Scotland-Yard

Editors of Encyclopaedia (2024 b, August 10). *Tower of London*. Encyclopedia Britannica. https://www.britannica.com/topic/Tower-of-London

Ehrlich, B., & Hebbert, M. J. (2017). London. In *Encyclopædia Britannica*. https://www.britannica.com/place/London

8 interesting facts about Westminster Abbey in London. (n.d.). London Tickets. https://www.london-tickets.co.uk/westminster-abbey/facts/

EssentialLDN. (2018, September 4). *London's most fascinating district - Whitechapel*. Essential History. https://essentiallldn.com/2018/09/04/londons-most-fascinating-district-whitechapel/

Facts Guy. (2022, June 14). *East London: 10 interesting facts you might not have known*. Interesting Facts. https://interestingfacts.co.za/geography/east-london/

Fun facts about the London Eye . (2022, December 19). Westminster and Changing of the Guard Tour. https://westminstertour.com/fun-facts-about-the-london-eye/

Getting around London. (n.d.). VisitLondon. https://www.visitlondon.com/traveller-information/getting-around-london

Guiberteau, O. (2019, August 9). *The baffling origin of London Stone*. BBC. https://www.bbc.com/travel/article/20190805-the-baffling-origin-of-london-stone

Guidelines To Britain. (2019, September 10). *10 facts about The British Museum in London*. https://guidelinestobritain.com/museums-art-galleries/facts-about-the-british-museum-in-london/

Holidify. (2023). *29 interesting facts about London*. https://www.holidify.com/pages/facts-about-london-6461.html

History of London Wall. (n.d.). English Heritage. https://www.english-heritage.org.uk/visit/places/london-wall/History/

Irvine, A. (2022, July 28). *Covent Garden*. History Hit. https://www.historyhit.com/locations/covent-garden/

Jarus, O. (2014, January 24). *Tower of London: Facts & history*. Live Science. https://www.livescience.com/42821-tower-of-london.html

Johnson, B. (n.d.). *London's Roman city wall walk*. Historic UK. https://www.historic-uk.com/HistoryMagazine/DestinationsUK/Londons-Roman-City-Wall/

Joyner, L. (2023, May 5). *13 fascinating facts about Westminster Abbey*. House Beautiful. https://www.housebeautiful.com/uk/lifestyle/property/g43619413/westminster-abbey-facts/

Kennedy, M. (2002, August 2). *Valuable Greek sculpture stolen*. The Guardian. https://www.theguardian.com/uk/2002/aug/02/education.arttheft

Kent, P. (2004, November 2). *Arts, briefly; Theft at the British Museum*. The New York Times. https://www.nytimes.com/2004/11/02/arts/arts-briefly-theft-at-the-british-museum.html

London facts for kids. (2015). Kiddle. https://kids.kiddle.co/London

London Wall facts for kids. (2023). Kiddle. https://kids.kiddle.co/London_Wall

London's lost rivers. (2019). GoParksLondon. https://www.goparks.london/articles/london-s-lost-rivers/

London's 8 weird and wonderful urban legends. (2019, March 10). A-Broad in London. https://a-broad-in-london.com/blog/2019/3/4/londons-8-weird-amp-wonderful-urban-legends-true-or-a-fantastic-tale

London Stone. (2023, July 22). City of London. https://www.thecityofldn.com/directory/london-stone/

London Tower Bridge fun facts. (2023, November 20). London Bridge. https://www.londonbridgetickets.com/fun-facts/

London Transport Museum. (n.d.). CoventGarden. https://www.coventgarden.london/experience/museums/london-transport-museum/

Mata, W. (2023, March 16). *Why London is technically a forest, according to the UN.* Evening Standard. https://www.standard.co.uk/news/london/london-technically-forest-united-nations-cambridge-dictionary-b1067877.html

Melbtravel. (2018, July 25). *Cool facts about Tower Bridge London England.* MelbTravel. https://www.melbtravel.com/cool-facts-tower-bridge-london-england/

Mike@bitaboutbritain. (2016, May 15). *The London Stone.* A Bit about Britain. https://bitaboutbritain.com/the-london-stone/

Millar, L. (17 C.E., April). *Your ultimate guide to visiting Warner Bros. Studio, London.* Get Your Guide. https://www.getyourguide.com/explorer/london-ttd57/visit-warner-bros-studio-london/

Mullens-Burgess, E. (2020, September 21). *Cabinet Office.* Institute for Government. https://www.instituteforgovernment.org.uk/explainer/cabinet-office

Myths and legends of the London Stone. (2023, September 17). A London Inheritance. https://alondoninheritance.com/london-history/myths-and-legends-of-the-london-stone/

9 surprising facts about the Tower of London moat. (n.d.). Historic Royal Palaces. https://www.hrp.org.uk/tower-of-london/history-and-stories/9-surprising-facts-about-the-tower-of-london-moat/#gs.dq66qg

ONS. (2021, November 29). *Religion, England and Wales: The religion of usual residents and household religious composition in England and wales, census 2021 data.* Office for National Statistics; Govt of UK. https://www.ons.gov.uk/peoplepopulationandcommunity/culturalidentity/religion/bulletins/religionenglandandwales/census2021

Our history. (2019). Warner Bros. Studio Tour London. https://www.wbstudiotour.co.uk/our-history/

Palace of Westminster facts for kids. (2015). Kiddle. https://kids.kiddle.co/Palace_of_Westminster

Plitt, A. (2015, August 10). *15 London Eye facts you didn't know.* Condé Nast Traveler. https://www.cntraveler.com/stories/2015-08-10/london-eye-things-you-didnt-know-tourist-attraction

Porter, L. (2017, August 11). *Houses of Parliament family guided tour review.* About London Laura. https://aboutlondonlaura.com/houses-parliament-family-guided-tour/

Rogers, J. (2015, December 10). *Myths and legends of London.* The Lost Byway. https://thelostbyway.com/2015/12/myths-and-legends-of-london.html

Rossen, J. (2021, September 12). *8 arresting facts about Scotland Yard.* Mental Floss. https://www.mentalfloss.com/article/550279/facts-about-scotland-yard-london-metropolitan-police

Scotland Yard facts for kids. (2016). Kiddle. https://kids.kiddle.co/Scotland_Yard

The secrets of Downing Street. (2022, October 27). Westminster and Changing of the Guard Tour. https://westminstertour.com/the-secrets-of-downing-street/

17 amazing facts about London Eye that will blow your mind. (n.d.). London Tickets - Headout. https://www.london-tickets.co.uk/london-eye-facts/

6 things you never knew about East London. (2017, November 17). Craft Gin Club. https://www.craftginclub.co.uk/ginnedmagazine/2017/11/17/6-things-you-never-knew-about-east-london

10 Downing Street facts for kids. (2015). Kiddle. https://kids.kiddle.co/10_Downing_Street#Cabinet_Room

10 facts about the Tower of London you never knew. (n.d.). The London Pass by Go City. https://londonpass.com/en/things-to-do/facts-about-the-tower-of-london

10 fascinating facts about Covent Garden, London. (2017, March 13). Britain and Britishness. https://britainandbritishness.com/10-fascinating-facts-about-covent-garden-london/

10 "horrible" facts about London! (2016, November 25). National Geographic Kids. https://www.natgeokids.com/uk/discover/history/general-history/ten-horrible-facts-about-london/

TfL Community Team. (2019, July 29). *Tube trivia and facts.* Made by TfL Blog. https://madeby.tfl.gov.uk/2019/07/29/tube-trivia-and-facts/

TfL Community Team. (2020, June 8). *The tramendous story behind London Trams.* Made by TfL Blog. https://madeby.tfl.gov.uk/2020/06/08/london-trams/

Things you might not know about Covent Garden. (n.d.). Covent Garden. https://www.coventgarden.london/cg-edit/things-you-might-not-know-about-covent-garden/

Top 10 facts about the City of London! (n.d.). Fun Kids. https://www.funkidslive.com/learn/top-10-facts/top-10-facts-about-the-city-of-london/

Top 10 facts about Parliament! (2022). Fun Kids. https://www.funkidslive.com/learn/top-10-facts/top-10-facts-about-parliament/

Top 10 facts about Royal Mail! (n.d.). Fun Kids. https://www.funkidslive.com/learn/top-10-facts/top-10-facts-about-royal-mail/

Transport for London. (2024, March 31). *Bus fleet data & audits.* Transport for London | Govt of UK. https://tfl.gov.uk/corporate/publications-and-reports/bus-fleet-data-and-audits

Transport for London. (n.d.). *Docklands Light Railway (DLR).* Transport for London. https://tfl.gov.uk/corporate/about-tfl/culture-and-heritage/londons-transport-a-history/dlr

Tucker, D. (2024, February 15). *The remarkable history of Covent Garden.* London Walks. https://www.walks.com/blog/covent-garden-history/

29 things you (probably) didn't know about the British Museum. (n.d.). The British Museum. https://www.britishmuseum.org/blog/29-things-you-probably-didnt-know-about-british-museum

UK Parliament. (n.d.). *His Majesty's government: The Cabinet - MPs and Lords*. Members.parliament.uk. https://members.parliament.uk/Government/Cabinet

Whitechapel facts for kids. (2021). Kiddle. https://kids.kiddle.co/Whitechapel

Whitehead, R., Brown, R., Harding , C., Brown, J., Gariban, S., & Moonen, T. (2020). *London at a crossroads: Chapter 2: London's economy and business*. Centre for London. https://centreforlondon.org/reader/london-crossroads/londons-economy-business/

Wignall, K. (2016, March 11). *Five historical things to look out for in... Whitechapel*. Time Out. https://www.timeout.com/london/blog/five-historical-things-to-look-out-for-in-whitechapel-031116

Wilde, E. (2023, February 25). *10 facts about the Tower of London*. Sterling Mint. https://sterlingmint.co.uk/2023/02/25/tower-of-london-10-facts/

Wood, P. (2019, February 14). *London is a forest*. The Street Tree. https://thestreettree.com/london-is-a-forest/#:~:text=In%20London%2C

ANNEXURE:

More Fun Places to Hang Out

Use this annexure to find additional places to chill out when in London. If you want some inside info on some of the best places to eat and entertain yourselves, then this is the section to read. The eateries mentioned here are kid-friendly, and many even have special kids' menus.

Places have been grouped under chapter titles so you know in which area to look for them. The subheadings should guide you about what you can do at these places. Remember though, London is full of great places to visit. This annexure is only a guide and does not claim to contain information on *all* the places you should or can visit.

Chapter 1: The Intruder at the Cabinet Office

Eateries

- **Old Shades Pub and Dining**, 37 Whitehall, is a traditional pub, constructed in 1898. This place has original ales too, though you may be too young to sample those. You can expect to find typically British food like steaks, pies, and soups. It would be best to book the place in advance.

- **Raffles Hotel**, OWO, Whitehall is located in the Old War Office of the city, the building in which legends and leaders like Winston Churchill and others made decisions for the country. Scenes of the *James Bond* movies were filmed here. The hotel offers a tour of the building in its signature "Tea and Tour" feature.

- **Tiroler Hut**, Westbourne Grove is an Austrian restaurant open since 1967. It serves great food, music with accordion and yodeling, and even its famed cowbell show.

- **Dear Jackie**, the Broadwick Soho, has grinning doormen in bowler hats, and it's known for its quirky, fun interiors as well as its lavish Italian spreads.

- **Brown's Hotel**, 33 Albemarle Street, Mayfair, is considered London's oldest luxury hotel established in 1832. Famous visitors like President Roosevelt, Mahatma Gandhi, Princess Diana, and writers like

Agatha Christie have all been guests here. This hotel grew brick by brick and is made up of 13 connected houses today.

Parks and Green Spots

- **Victoria Tower Gardens** is a public park along the Thames, next to Victoria Tower, one of the South West towers of the Palace of Westminster. It extends from the palace to Lambeth Bridge. It is also known for its magnificent monuments and statues. Some things in the park that you may enjoy viewing are:
    - The Buxton Memorial Fountain
    - a stone wall with a statue of a goat and two kids
    - a statue of the suffragette, Emmeline Pankhurst, who fought for women's voting rights in 1918.

Fun, Entertainment, and Education

- **Banqueting House**, Whitehall, City of Westminster: This is the only survivor of the Palace of Whitehall. It was used as a museum and chapel in the past and hosted elaborate masques (dances in masks). Take special note of the ceiling painted by the great artist Peter Paul Rubens. It is the largest of his work in its original location in Europe. Tours of the place are available. Please note that it will only open in 2025 after renovations.

- **The London Dungeon**, County Hall, Westminster Bridge Road, South Bank: This horror-comedy tourist attraction of the country's gruesome and bloody past uses live actors, costumes, stage settings, props, and rides to offer thrills, chills, and laughs. The only thing to keep in mind is the age limit. Children below five years are not permitted, and the recommended age for others is above 12. Anyone under 16 needs to be accompanied by an adult.

- **The Graffiti Tunnel**, or **Leake Street Arches**, are eight former railway arches below Waterloo station that were reclaimed as the longest graffiti wall. It also has restaurants, bars, and pubs.

Chapter 2: Why Is the Future of London City in Jeopardy?

Eateries

- **The street food market** around the Leadenhall Building, 122 Leadenhall Street (also known as the "Cheese grater" because it looks just like that), is a foodie paradise you should not miss. You will find burgers, tacos, and curries—you name it.

Parks and Green Spots

- **Carter Lane Gardens** in St. Paul's Churchyard is a green spot in the city if you want to catch up with friends and family or enjoy the greens and a picnic lunch.

Fun, Entertainment, and Education

- **Barbican Conservatory**, Silk Street, is a glass-roofed conservatory for tropical plants, trees, birdlife, and exotic fish.

- **Leadenhall Market**, Gracechurch Street, is a covered market known for its food and shopping centers. The Leaky Cauldron pub scenes from *Harry Potter* were filmed here.

- **Parents Paradise Children's Play Centre**, Unit C, Greatham Road Industrial Estate, Greatham Rd, Watford: This children's amusement park offers soft play for kids up to the age of 11. It has a lot of options for climbing frames, slides, tunnels, and rides for children apart from other excitements.

- **The Atria**, Watford: This amazing glass-roofed shopping mall gives you the chance to shop and eat to your heart's content.

- **The Lookout,** 8 Bishopsgate's 50th-floor viewing gallery, gives you a view of the city's iconic landmarks, impressive skyscrapers, and historic architecture without any admission fee.

- **St Botolph-without-Bishopsgate** is an early 18th-century church that you can explore if you like the quiet charms of the city. Though this particular church has been rebuilt, the earlier church on the site existed as early as 1212.

- **The Old Bailey,** or the Central Criminal Court of England and Wales, is where some of the most sensational cases in English history were fought. You can see a live court session too. The building built in the 1870s is grand. However, no cameras or recording devices are allowed within it.

Chapter 3: The Mystery of the Trapped Tourists

Eateries

- **Great Scotland Yard Hotel**, on Scotland Yard Street, is a luxury hotel owned by the Hyatt group. It is in the building that was the headquarters of the Metropolitan force. You can still see the iconic red brick wall, Portland stone, and green doors so famously part of the police department in the 1870s.

- **The Ivy**, between Litchfield and West Streets, was founded in 1917 and is particularly known as the haunt of Westend theater-goers, actors, and celebrities. It has a club for artists where a membership is extremely hard to get. This club has a private and secret entrance via a nearby flower shop!

- **Henrietta Hotel**, Henrietta Street, is known for its fun and quirky decor combining traditional Covent Garden, Italian, and 1970s style elements. Having opened only in 2017, the restaurant serves English, French, and continental cuisine.

- **Neal's Yard** in Seven Dials is a colorful courtyard of eateries, shopping areas, and other places perfect for walking around and exploring. Seven Dials itself is unique for its star-shaped layout, originally designed in the 1690s, and is a great place for various types of foods—Asian, British, continental, and more.

Parks and Green Spots

- **Diamond Jubilee Garden**, The Embankment, Twickenham, is a park and green spot very close to Covent Garden that has a play area, a cafe, and an area for fencing. You may not know this, but this park was once a swimming pool and has retained some of its original features!

Fun, Entertainment, and Education

- **Street Performers:** Covent Garden is a great place to catch jugglers, magicians, and other street performers at all times of the year. This is a great hit with kids.

- **The Royal Opera House**, Bow Street, has special family sessions on Sundays where you can explore not just the venue but also the artists and opera and ballet performances. There are interactive and fun activities too.

- **Kids' plays** at the Drury Lane Theater or the Lyceum on Wellington Street like *Frozen* and *The Lion King* ensure that plays need not all be serious or for the grownups.

- **The Bow Street Police Museum** is located where the Magistrates Court and the Police Station of the 19th century once stood. You can learn all about law and order and its men in the city!

Chapter 4: The Mystery of Saving the British Monarchy

Eateries

- **City Spice**, Brick Lane, is the perfect joint for Bangladeshi food. It is located in a former sari (the ethnic flowy garment worn by women of the Indian subcontinent) shop, which was closed down. Try out the special "staff curry" if you can tolerate the spice! There are other curry places in the area like The Monsoon and Aladin, which serve Indian, Pakistani, and Bangladeshi food.

- **Beigel Bake** on Brick Lane offers yummy bagels that are slightly chewier than their American counterparts. There are eye-opening varieties of what you would think is just a classic dish at this Jewish bakery.

- **Poppies Fish and Chips**, Hanbury Street, is one of the best places for fish and chips in the city. The owner has been in the business of serving this delicacy since he was a kid!

- **The English Restaurant**, Crispin Street is a 17th-century establishment with dim lighting and wooden floors. It serves the traditional English dessert of bread and butter pudding among various other delicacies.

- **Old Spitalfields Market** is the perfect place for street food and stalls where you will find all sorts of global food under one roof!

Parks and Green Spots

- **Tower Hill Garden** near the Tower of London is a small garden and park which has a kids play area as well.

- **St Dustan-in-the-East** on St Dunstan's Hill was a church that was bombed and destroyed in WWII. However, the gardens planted in the ruins are open to the public and are a sight to behold.

- **Sky Garden**, 20 Fenchurch Street, has London's highest public garden atop a building and is also known as "the walkie-talkie" for its unique shape. Though there is no entrance fee, book in advance to visit because seats are limited.

- **The Garden at 120**, 120 Fenchurch Street, has London's largest public rooftop space and is free to visit without any booking required

Fun, Entertainment, and Education

- **HMS Belfast**, in the Pool of London on the River Thames, was a vessel used by the Royal Navy, built in 1936, but is now permanently moored as a museum ship. She saw active service in WWII and was put out of service in 1963. You can learn more about life on the sea and the inner workings of the ship.

- **Tate Modern**, Bankside, is one of the largest modern art galleries in the world and highlights the work of modern artists. There are no fees to view the permanent collection, but there is one for the temporary exhibitions.

- **Jack the Ripper Museum**, Cable Street is the ultimate location if you want to know everything about the unknown serial killer, including his victims, areas of operation, and everything in between! It is a five-room exhibition that has a police station from the era and a fake morgue with shrines in honor of the five victims. There is no age limit here, and children above eight years are charged.

- **Pelican Stairs**, near Wapping, is an alleyway that leads to a secret beach in London. Hereabouts you will also find a pub from 1520, The Prospect of Whitby, also nicknamed "The Devil's Tavern."

Chapter 5: Uncovering the Secret Underground Drug Transport in London

Eateries

- **Langham**, Portland Place, Regent Street, is a 5-star hotel that has been in existence since the 1860s. It has a Palm Court that continues to serve tea from the olden days. Artur Conan Doyle set at least two of his *Sherlock Holmes* stories partly in the Langham!

- **Old Compton Brasserie**, 40 Museum Street, Soho, established in 2018, has great food and drinks in an old-fashioned atmosphere. The place also exhibits art by local artists.

Parks and Green Spots

- **Hyde Park** in Westminster is one of the largest public parks in the city. It has a Speaker's Corner where people can openly talk about any subject under the sun. It has also hosted several concerts of famous music bands like Queen, Rolling Stones, and Pink Floyd.

- **Regent's Park**, Westminster, is a public park open from 5 a.m. to 9 p.m. It has rowboats, a small theater, and plenty of nature to soak in.

- **London Zoo**, in a part of Regent's Park, is the oldest scientific zoo in the world. The Tower of London menagerie was transferred here in 1832. It also has one of the world's largest collections of animals and birds.

Fun, Entertainment, and Education

- **Kynance Mews**, South Kensington, is stunningly beautiful for photos or selfies with a backdrop of nature and historic architecture.

- **Word on the Water**, Regent's Canal Towpath, is a floating bookstore near King's Cross. It is on a 1920s Dutch canal boat named Dianti.

- **Madame Tussauds**, Marylebone Road, is the best and one of the oldest wax museums in the world. It has a large collection of 150 life-size wax statues of celebrities, Royal family members, and others.

- **The Shard**, near London Bridge, is a 72-story skyscraper, which is the tallest building in the UK. It has a glass viewing gallery and an open-air observation deck that offers a spectacular view of the city.

- **Natural History Museum**, Cromwell Rd, South Kensington is a museum that houses earth and life science specimens related to collections in botany (study of plants), zoology (study of animals), entomology (study of insects), paleontology (study of life before the Holocene Period roughly 11,700 years ago), and mineralogy (study of minerals).

- **Selfridges**, 400 Oxford St, Marylebone, a department store established in 1908, is as well-known for the products they sell as for the architecture of the shops and their elaborate and eye-catching window displays.

- **Liberty**, Great Marlborough Street, is a luxury department store established in 1875. The store is known for men's, women's, and children's fashion clothes. The building is just as spectacular because it forms a three-story archway over the northern entrance to the Kingly Street Mall where the Liberty Clock is.

- **SEA Life London Aquarium**, County Hall, on the South Bank of the River Thames, is not far from Buckingham Palace. It has glass tunnels where you can view every sort of water creature. It also has a penguin exhibit, which might be fun.

Printed in Great Britain
by Amazon